THE
SALTWATER
FISH

I D E N T I F I E R

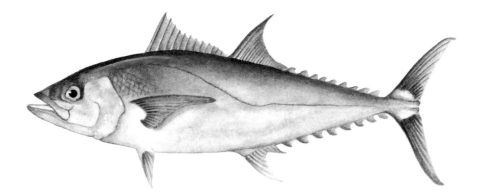

THE
SALTWATER
FISH
IDENTIFIER

AL RISTORI

MALLARD
PRESS

MALLARD PRESS

An imprint of BDD Promotional
Book Company, Inc.
666 Fifth Avenue, New York, NY 10103

Mallard Press and its accompanying design and
logo are trademarks of
BDD Promotional Book Company, Inc.

First published in the United States of America
in 1992 by the Mallard Press

ISBN 0-7924-5575-4

This book was designed and produced by
Quintet Publishing Limited
6 Blundell Street
London N7 9BH

Creative Director: Terry Jeavons
Designer: Chris Dymond
Project Editor: Lindsay Porter
Editor: Rosemary Booton
Illustrator: Sharon Bailey

Typeset in Great Britain by
Central Southern Typesetters, Eastbourne
Manufactured in Singapore by Eray Scan (Pte) Ltd
Printed in Hong Kong by
Leefung-Asco Printers Limited

Contents

Introduction

Welcome to the wonderful world of saltwater fish. The diversity of the underwater world which occupies most of our planet has fascinated me ever since I was a youngster, and I hope this book will inspire you just as others peaked my interest in both fishing and marine biology.

There are probably over 20,000 species of fish in the world (scientific estimates vary greatly, and new species are still being discovered), with about 60 per cent residing in salt waters. However, the diversity in North American waters isn't quite that great. The American Fisheries Society listed 2,268 species in their 1980 list, which was up from 1,872 species in the list published just 20 years prior to that.

In setting up this volume, I departed from the usual format of fish identification books. Rather than classifying species strictly by family, I've broken them down into the broad areas where they're most likely to be found. This is intended to make it easier for

ABOVE: Capt Bob Montgomery gaffs a cobia off Key West. More of the fish circle the boat, curiously waiting for a bait or a lure.

BELOW: The adult African pompano loses all the streamers on its dorsal and anal fins which makes it difficult to believe the juvenile is the same species.

those using the guide to find a species. For instance, if you're a New York angler who wants to know more about the blackfish, it's only necessary to glance through the species directory under "Atlantic Coolwater Inshore Species". This way you can determine that the species you know by its local name is actually the tautog, a member of the largely tropical wrasse family.

Unfortunately, the dividing line between Atlantic warmwater and coolwater species is far from exact. The former are primarily species which are most abundant south of Cape Hatteras, North Carolina. However, many species listed there (such as king mackerel, cobia, amberjack, spotted seatrout and spot) are also very common in the Chesapeake Bay area – and the black drum has a northernmost spawning area in Delaware Bay. These and many other warmwater species may range far north during the summer, when water temperatures rise into the seventies up through the southern side of Cape Cod.

Many of the coolwater species will also range south. The weakfish is most abundant from Virginia to Cape Cod, and is thus classified with the northern species. However, it's also common to the south and even moves into the Gulf of Mexico. The bluefish ranges even further (from Maine well into the Gulf of Mexico), but is also classified with the coolwater fish because the vast majority of the catch is taken between Cape Cod and Cape Hatteras.

Unfortunately, space prevents us from listing all species, or even from illustrating every one described. Virtually all of those which are important as game and food fish are included. However we had to omit some of the interesting, but only occasionally hooked, species as well as those species which serve primarily as forage fish and

ABOVE: A sandbar shark with a tag implanted.

bait, such as balao, menhaden, smelt, anchovies, sardines, flyingfish, needlefish, killifish, silversides, mullet and butterfish.

Anadromous species present a special problem. These are fish which spend most of their lives at sea but return to fresh waters in order to spawn. By tradition, those species which have short life-spans (often returning only once to spawn before dying) or are caught by anglers primarily while in fresh waters are treated as freshwater fish – even though the vast majority of their lives are spent in salt waters. Thus, the salmons, steelhead rainbow trout, sturgeons, and American shad have not been included – while the striped bass is featured in the "Atlantic Coolwater Inshore Species" section despite the fact that it is found in all three areas and has been introduced into land-locked fresh waters throughout much of the United States.

ABOVE: A sandbar shark with a tag implanted.

LEFT: The author with a snook, a species which displays a prominent lateral line.

It is most important that the reader study Chapter 2 before going on to the descriptions of fishes. That chapter includes information about how fish are classified and their various parts which provide identification. In many cases there are only a few clues which separate one species from another, and those reading this book should be able to surprise even some "old salts" by making those distinctions.

Classification and Identification of Fishes

Fish are identified by class, order, family, subfamily, tribe, genus, and species. There are only three classes – Agnatha (jawless fishes), Chondrichthyes (cartilaginous fishes), and Osteichthyes (bony fishes).

To take an example, sharks have cartilage rather than bone, and thus fall into the class Chondrichthyes. There are many orders (*formes* endings) reflecting basic anatomical differences. For instance, the shortfin mako (*Isurus oxyrinchus*) is part of the order Squaliformes, which includes the familiar-shaped sharks and separates them from the orders Hexanchiformes (frill and cow sharks), Heterodontiformes (bullhead sharks), Rajiformes (sawfishes, guitarfishes, rays, and skates) and Chimaeriformes (chimaeras).

Within Squaliformes, the shortfin mako belongs to the family Lamnidae (mackerel sharks). That family includes the similar longfin mako, porbeagle, white and salmon sharks – but to illustrate the broadness of family groupings which the layman can hardly hope to understand, the plankton-eating basking shark is also included in the same family.

In order to modify such confusion, the family can be further broken down into subfamily, tribe, and genus. Thus, the tunas belong to the largest class, Ostiechthyes

ABOVE: The mako shark cannot be mistaken for any other because of the curvature of its protruding teeth.

LEFT: The characteristic barred markings of the wahoo are clearly shown.

(bony fishes) and the order Perciformes. The family Scombridae (mackerels) is broken down into the subfamilies Scombrinae and the single species Gasterochismatinae (the butterfly kingfish, found only in the southern hemisphere). The tribes of the Scrombinae are the tunas (Thunnini), bonitos (Sardini), Spanish mackerels or seerfishes (Scomberomorini), and mackerels (Scombrini). The tuna tribe features the primary genus

Thunnas (including the bluefin, yellowfin, bigeye, blackfin, and albacore), but there are also the *Euthynnus* (little tunny, kawakawa and black skipjack), *Katsuwonus* (skipjack), and *Auxis* (bullet and frigate mackerels). These are tunas despite the name.

Every fish has Latin names which are used by scientists throughout the world. The zoological system of identifying species of fish is well established, but that doesn't mean that scientific names never change. There's always some infighting within the scientific community, and changes occur from time to time. For instance, the scientific name probably best known by sportfishers was that of the striped bass – but *Roccus saxatilis* was changed to *Morone saxatilis* a couple of decades ago. The first letter of the first word in the Latin name (the genus) is always capitalized, but the second name (the species) is not.

There is relative stability in scientific names, which serves to cut through confusion associated with common names used in different areas of the country and, in many cases, the world. In every case, our guide for this volume has been the standards laid down by the American Fisheries Society in their Special Publication No. 12, "A List of Common and Scientific Names of Fishes from the United States and Canada" (Fourth Edition, 1980).

The selection of common names by the Society follows a series of guidelines. Simplicity in names is favored, and common names are not capitalized in text except when a proper name is involved, such as Spanish mackerel. What the Society sought were "colorful, romantic, fanciful, metaphorical, and otherwise distinctive and original names" plus those of American Indian (tautog, menhaden) and immigrant origin

(such as the Italian bocaccio and Spanish grouper, cero, barracuda, and pompano).

Structural attributes, color, and pattern as well as ecological characteristics (such as tripletail, copper, mottled, sand, etc) are appropriate for common names, and geographic references (southern, northern, Arctic) are fine as long as they are accurate. The duplication of common names for fishes and other organisms should be avoided, but names in wide general use are not rejected on that basis alone. Thus, the dolphin retains its name despite the confusion with the mammal of the same name.

Identification

Now that we know what to call them, the next problem is identifying the species. There are many clues to fish identification. Form is the first thing to consider. No one could mistake the flattened appearance of the flounders, rays, and skates, or the snake-like body of the eels with the normal compressed fish body, which is flattened from side to side. Within the latter are the more rounded and streamlined species such as the tunas and mackerels.

While form is a good clue in many cases, and one which doesn't vary much from individual to individual within a species, there are many families of fish with almost identical outward appearances. Coloration is the next easy-to-spot consideration, but this can be extremely variable in such species as the groupers. Many fish change

LEFT: The yellowfin, like other tunas, has a lunate caudal fin (tail) and slim caudal penduncle. (See illustration on page 12 for anatomical terms.)

BELOW: Little tunny readily hit small lures retrieved at high speed.

color as they get excited, or when over different bottom. For instance, flounders may be very light-colored over sand but dark when living on mud. The general habitat can also make a big difference. Migrating striped bass often have a purplish sheen on the back which they lose after entering bays and rivers, while those living their lives in rivers tend to have a greenish tint. To top it off, only the dullest of fish don't change color much when they die.

Yet, color pattern can often be a very good clue. Stripes and bars may vary slightly in number, width, and intensity of color, but usually are solid identification factors. Look for markings on the body which will always be there regardless of a color variation. For instance, the black saddle at the base of the Nassau grouper's tail is a sure clue in any color phase.

BELOW: The author with a female dolphin. This fish could not be mistaken for any other on coloration alone.

Most fishes are propelled through the water by body movement starting with the tail, or caudal fin, and the area immediately forward of it which is referred to as the caudal peduncle. The other fins basically act as stabilizing and maneuvring devices. However, fishes with rigid bodies must use their fins for swimming and a few – such as triggerfish and trunkfish – can be surprisingly fast in short bursts.

Tail shapes easily separate various groups. For instance, the speedy tunas have lunate tails, while the almost-as-fast jacks have a wider falcate tail. Both families also feature narrow caudal peduncles. On the other

ABOVE: The black saddle patch of the Nassau grouper is a sure identification feature in any color phase.

hand, the more sedentary, bottom-dwelling groupers sport a truncate, broom-like tail with a thick caudal peduncle. Within each family there may be variations in tail shape which helps to separate the species. Color and markings on the fins are also very important, as that may be the easiest clue with many similar species.

Fin placement and configuration is a solid clue. The normal arrangement in a bony fish consists of a spiny first dorsal fin on the back which is followed by a soft-rayed second dorsal. The anal fin is usually soft-

ABOVE: The queen triggerfish is a gaudy species with leather-like skin and a first dorsal which locks into place but can be retracted by "triggering" the small second spine. These fish are quite strong despite their relatively rigid bodies.

LEFT: Capt Joe Alexander with a black grouper which has the straight, truncate caudal fin and broad caudal peduncle typical of this bottom dwelling family. (See illustration on page 12 for anatomical terms).

RIGHT: The jack family, which includes this permit caught at Key West by the author, have falcate caudal fins.

BELOW: The pectoral fins of rays are modified into "wings" with which they "fly" through the water.

rayed, but may have a few spiny rays at the base. The pelvic or ventral fins are located on the lower body, usually just below the pectoral fin. However, in more primitive fish such as the herring, the pelvic fins are well to the rear, and they're missing completely in a few species, such as swordfish and eels. Pectoral fins are located just aft of the gill cover, and their length is a sure identifier of the albacore and some other species. Pectorals are greatly modified into the meaty wings of skates and rays, and slightly modified to provide feelers for sea robins and the wings of flying fish which actually allow them to glide in the air for considerable

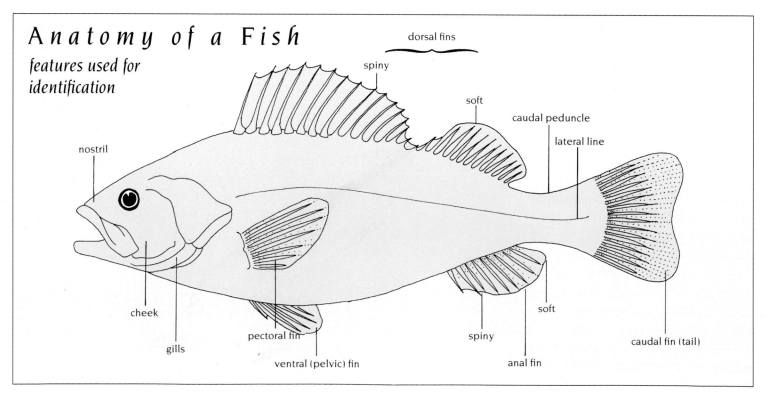

Anatomy of a Fish
features used for identification

dorsal fins

spiny

soft

caudal peduncle

lateral line

nostril

cheek

gills

pectoral fin

ventral (pelvic) fin

spiny

anal fin

soft

caudal fin (tail)

LEFT: The striped sea robin (below) and northern sea robin (above) have modified pectoral fins which serve as feelers for feeding on the bottom.

BELOW: The crevalle lack has scutes on the caudal peduncle which are typical of the jack family.

distances. Check the illustration so you're familiar with all the fins, as their placement is critical in identifying some similar species.

The bodies of almost all fishes are covered by scales and mucus. The scales aren't often a major identifying factor, but the jacks have distinctive scutes at the caudal peduncle which are formed by large scales. Sharks have a rough skin composed of tiny placoid scales which are similar in origin to their teeth. That's why the skin feels like sandpaper when you rub toward the head. Most catfish have scaleless bodies, but eels have scales which can only be seen under a microscope.

There are many more exterior signs, such as the shape of the head, placement of the eyes, type of mouth, scaled or unscaled gill plate, etc. Only in a few cases may it be necessary to go any further for an identification. With sharks the best clue is often the unique teeth of a species. Other fish may, or may not, have some type of teeth – and a few species (such as some grunts) have brightly colored mouths. Gill raker counts will separate most species, and are particularly good with the similar-appearing tunas. As a last resort, one can check the internal organs. In the case of the tunas there are smooth and striated livers which separate some species.

All fish begin life as an egg (roe) which must be fertilized by the male's sperm (referred to as milt). Ironically, in the case of almost all "more advanced" bony fishes, fertilization is external, whereas most of the "primitive" sharks copulate, with the female producing live young which are able to fend for themselves immediately upon birth. In most cases it's impossible to determine the sex of fish externally, but male sharks which fertilize internally have prominent claspers which they insert into the female. Male blue sharks also retain a hold on the females (who have thicker skins) with their teeth, and it's easy to spot all the white scars on even free-swimming females. In a few other cases, males or females of a species will acquire a specific characteristic (such as the blueish hump on the head of an adult male black sea bass) or they may be colored differently. Sex reversal occurs in the sea bass family, Serranidae, with the groupers and other species starting life as females and later transforming into males as they grow.

Habitat Key

The following definitions refer to the habitat categories used in the Species Directory.

Inshore waters: ocean waters within 20 miles of the shore, or the continental shelf, if nearer.

Offshore waters: ocean waters from 20 miles of the shore, up to the end of the continental shelf.

Oceanic waters: depths of over 100 fathoms or beyond the continental shelf.

Wrecks: wrecked ships or any sheltered environment.

Fishing terms

The tips on angling include the following terms:

Chumming: the process of using ground or chopped bait to attract fish to the boat.

Trolling: running baits or lures astern of a moving boat.

Light tackle: tackle which is comparably "light" for the size and the power of the fish being sought. Thus, while an ultralight outfit with 2lb mono would be "light" for Atlantic mackerel, an 80lb class big game outfit would also be "light" for giant bluefin tuna.

Heavy tackle: generally referring to big game, trolling or very heavy bottom fishing tackle, but also to any tackle which is heavier than necessary for the size and power of the fish targeted.

Fishing associations

The National Marine Fisheries Service (NMFS) is the US government agency primarily concerned with marine fisheries research and management. Most important food and sport species have been placed under some sort of management plan in recent years, and those not covered are certain to be regulated in the future.

The International Game Fish Association (IGFA) was established in 1939, to serve as a central processing center for world record data, and to establish ethical international angling regulations. The IGFA issues publications and has a public library with over 8,000 books on fish and fishing, plus films and works of art. Individual memberships are encouraged.

For details contact: *The International Game Association, 3000 E. Las Olas Blvd, Fort Lauderdale, FL, 33316-1616 (305 467-0161)*

Oceanic Species

The most majestic of all fish are the billfish. True oceanic wanderers, they have more than their unique bills in common. All are outstanding leapers, and rank among the great fighting fish of the world. For most anglers, catching a billfish of any kind is the experience of a lifetime, and even veterans who have caught hundreds experience that old thrill when a bill appears behind a trolled bait or lure. The billfish family includes

THE BILLFISH FAMILY
Istiophoridae

the marlins, sailfish and spearfish. The swordfish may appear similar in basic configuration, but it is classified in an entirely different family, Xiphiidae – of which it is the only member.

A federal billfish management plan prohibits the commercial capture of marlin, sailfish and spearfish from the western North Atlantic, and also their sale in the US without a valid import permit to prove they were taken from an area where their capture is legal. Minimum sizes for retention by sportfishers in the management plan area as of 1990 were (measured from the lower jaw to the fork of the tail) 86in (218cm) for blue marlin, 62in (157cm) for white marlin, and 57in (145cm) for sailfish.

BELOW: Peter Foley works a tagged blue marlin by the bill in order to revive it after a long fight

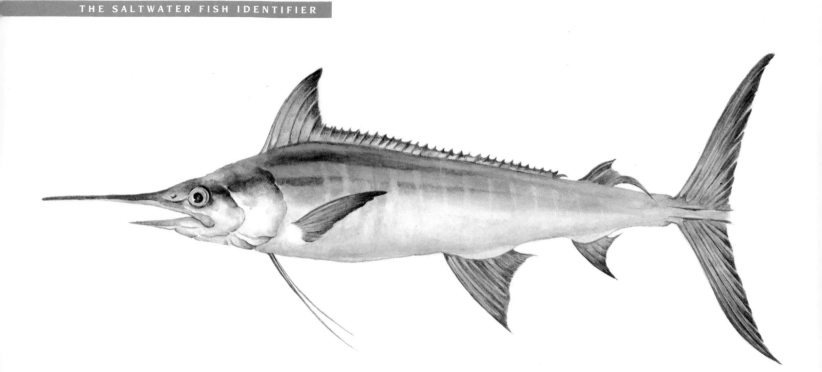

Blue Marlin

Makaira nigricans

Though the IGFA keeps separate records for both the Atlantic and Pacific blue marlin, most marine biologists classify them under the same scientific name or consider the two populations as subspecies. Japanese longline records indicate that the blue grows to even greater sizes than the closely related black marlin, though the long-standing IGFA black marlin record of 1,560lb (708kg) caught off Cabo Blanco, Peru by Alfred C Glassell, Jr in 1953, was larger than the blue marlin standards as of 1990. Actually, a blue of 1,805lb (819kg) was caught on rod and reel off Hawaii in 1972, but isn't recognized officially because more than one angler fought the fish.

The blue has a dorsal fin which is high and pointed anteriorly (rather than rounded, as in the white marlin) and there are no spots in the fins – as are usually present in the dorsals of the white and striped marlin. The back is cobalt blue, while the flanks and belly are silvery white. Blue vertical stripes are usually present on the sides, but aren't nearly as prominent as in the striped marlin – and often fade away completely after death.

Blue marlin feed on any oceanic live bait fish which they can catch, and the largest

---

DATA

Habitat: Oceanic waters.

Habits: Surface feeder.

Range: Atlantic – Massachusetts to Florida, Bermuda, Bahamas, Caribbean, and Gulf of Mexico. Pacific – Hawaii, and from Baja California south.

Size: Average 200–500lb (91–227kg); up to over 2,000lb (908kg). All very large blue marlin are females, and males rarely exceed 300lb (136kg).

---

specimens have been known to capture tuna of over 100lb (45kg). Almost all blues caught by sportfishing are taken by trolling live or dead baits or high-speed lures with 50 to 80lb tackle. However, the biggest threat to the species comes from longliners which now work throughout its range. The flesh is good-eating, and brings a high price in Japan and Hawaii – while also being a staple food in countries throughout its range, except in the United States. Most anglers now tag and

release all but trophy blues and those to be weighed in for tournaments.

The Atlantic blue marlin ranges the ocean from 45° N to 35° S. It can be caught as far north as Massachusetts by anglers fishing the eastern canyons, though the northern limit of reasonable abundance may be considered to be Baltimore and Wilmington Canyons. However, while relatively few blues are encountered in the northerly canyons, some of the largest specimens are taken from those waters – with the State records for New Jersey and New York both well over 1,000lb (454kg). The prime area for the Atlantic blue along the American coast is around Cape Hatteras, NC, where the Gulf Stream comes within about 20 miles (32km) of shore. Charter boats fishing out of Hatteras and Oregon Inlets catch hundreds of blue marlin each year and, fortunately, most are now released.

A very similar species in the Pacific is the black marlin (*Makaira indicus*), but there is no problem involved in distinguishing these look-alikes. As is the case with most fish, the blue's pectoral fins fold back against its body; however, the black marlin has rigid pectorals which cannot be bent back.

White Marlin

Tetrapturus albidus

The smallest of the marlin may well be the best fighter on a pound-for-pound basis. Easily overwhelmed on standard marlin tackle, this species is an excellent game fish when hooked on 20 to 30lb gear. The white is easily distinguished from the other billfish by the rounded, rather than pointed, tip of the first dorsal fin as well as the rounded pectoral and anal fins. There may also be a scattering of black or purple spots on the first dorsal and anal fins. Whites vary in color, but are generally lighter than other marlin – and often show light blue vertical bars on the flanks when alive.

Though found in the same range of the Atlantic as the blue, the white tends to move much further inshore. At one time they were commonly encountered during July in Butterfish Hole, only 12 miles (19km) off Montauk Point, Long Island – and a large charter fleet built up at Ocean City, Md because of the great white marlin fishing discovered in 1935 at the Jack Spot, 24 miles (38km) southeast of the inlet – in depths of only 50–60ft (15–18m).

Unfortunately, those inshore fisheries have disappeared with the increase in long-lining. However, though the best fishing is now concentrated in the canyons, whites are still likely to be encountered as strays in relatively near-shore areas by anglers trolling for such species as school bluefin tuna – and in 30–40 fathom areas somewhat inshore of the canyons. Whites are most abundant from Wilmington Canyon, Del-

---

DATA

Habitat: Offshore to oceanic waters.

Habits: Surface feeder.

Range: Atlantic coast north to Cape Cod; Gulf of Mexico; Caribbean.

Size: Average 40–60lb (18–27kg); up to almost 200lb (91kg).

---

aware, south, with good fishing from such ports as Cape May, NJ, Ocean City, Md, and Virginia Beach, Va.

Most white marlin are taken by trolling baits (especially balao) or high-speed lures. Live scup and other small fish are cast to surfacing whites with excellent results by New England sportsfishers. Large whites often take dead baits being fished for sharks or tuna. Whites aren't rated highly as a fresh food fish, but are considered to be a good species for smoking.

BELOW: A white marlin which had a line tangled around its tail, is lifted aboard a charter boat prior to release.

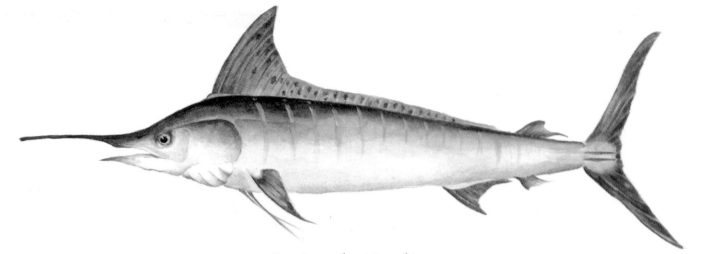

Striped Marlin

Tetrapturus audax

Striped marlin are distinguished by their high, pointed first dorsal fin, which normally equals or exceeds the greatest body depth. The sides are more compressed than those of the blue, and the blueish vertical stripes are very prominent – even after death. The fins of this species have irridescent blue spots, and the fins themselves often turn a neon blue when the fish is excited. Striped marlin are great game fish on appropriate tackle (30lb is ideal) and tend to jump far more than heavier blues and blacks.

The most common marlin in many temperate and tropical waters of the Pacific and Indian Oceans, the striped marlin provides Californians with a July-through-October marlin fishery. Though they have been known to range as far north as Oregon,

---

DATA

Habitat: Offshore to oceanic waters.

Habits: Surface feeder.

Range: In the eastern Pacific from southern California to Peru; also Hawaii.

Size: Average 100–200lb (45–90kg); up to 500lb (227kg) in western Pacific.

---

this is basically a southern California fishery. The finest striped marlin fishing occurs on both sides of the Baja California, especially at Cabo San Lucas in the winter and spring – though winter water temperatures may

be only in the mid-sixties (around 18°C). Striped marlin are only occasionally caught in the warm waters along the Central American coast, but are abundant closer to the cooling Humboldt Current off Ecuador. The largest of all are caught off New Zealand.

Whereas other marlin are usually caught by blind trolling, striped marlin tend to "tail" in the warm surface waters and can be spotted before baits are presented to them. The traditional dead balao will interest some of them, but live mackerel and other small live fish trolled or cast are the best bet. High-speed trolling with artificials also produces striped marlin.

This species has red meat which is not highly desired as food, but it is used in Japan and many other countries.

Longbill Spearfish

Tetrapturus pfluegeri

Spearfish are the smallest and most unusual of the billfish. They appear to be somewhat of a cross between a white marlin and a sailfish, but with the bill practically broken off. Spearfish catches are quite unusual, but this may be because they tend to frequent waters further from the continental shelf. Three species are recognized by marine scientists, the others being the shortbill (T. *angustirostris*) and the Mediterranean (T. *belone*). The shortbill is a Pacific species which is occasionally taken off

---

DATA

Habitat: Oceanic waters.

Habits: Surface feeder.

Range: Atlantic coast south of Cape Cod and into the Gulf of Mexico.

Size: Average 30–40lb (13–18kg); up to 100lb (45kg).

Hawaii, and has a bill which is hardly longer than its lower jaw. The longbill's is twice as long, but is still comparatively shorter than that of other billfish.

Spearfish have slender bodies and can be distinguished at a glance by the location of the vent forward of the anal fin – rather than close to it as in all other billfish. The IGFA keeps one set of records for all spearfish, and several line-test marks have been set off Hawaii. Long-lining or trolling are the best methods for catching longbills.

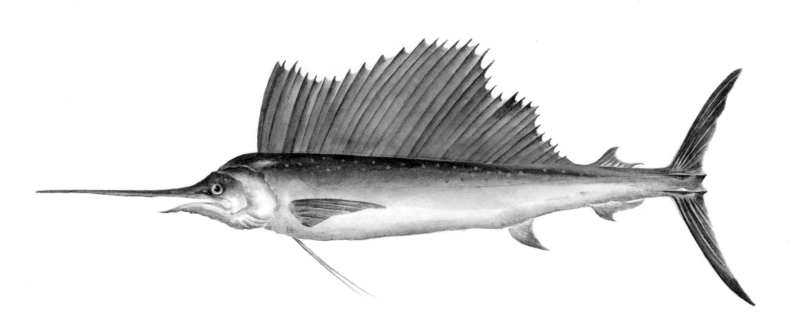

Sailfish

Istiophorus platypterus

DATA

Habitat: Inshore to offshore waters.

Habits: Surface feeder.

Range: Atlantic coast south of Cape Cod and into the Gulf of Mexico and Caribbean. Pacific – Baja California to Peru.

Size: Atlantic – average 30–50lb (13–23kg); up to over 125lb (54kg). Pacific – average 90–125lb (40–54kg), up to over 200lb (90kg).

Though there's a great disparity In size between Atlantic and Pacific sailfish, scientists consider them to be the same species. The huge sail-like dorsal fin provides instant identification. It is generally bluish, and covered with scattered black spots.

Atlantic sails are fine game fish when taken on very light tackle. They provide a major fishery when they concentrate off Florida's south-east coast in the winter, often working together to herd baitfish into a ball before attacking them. This usually occurs during northerly blows and rough seas from December to February, and is known as "balling the bait." At such times, sailfish are often caught and released by the dozens as anglers simply flip baits to the "turned on" sails. However, the usual methods involve trolling dead baits or very slow trolling live blue runners, balao or similar small live baits. Sails are also caught on a variety of trolled artificials.

Sails migrate north along the Atlantic coast in the summer, and fair numbers are hooked off Hatteras. However, they become quite unusual north of there, and are almost never caught above Virginia. Unlike the marlins, Atlantic sails prefer relatively shallow waters along the coasts, staying on the edge of the Gulf Stream and spreading well inshore over the reef. Some are even caught from ocean piers in Florida. However, in the Gulf of Mexico they stay well offshore in the Loop Current.

In addition to south-east Florida, there is excellent sailfishing off the Yucatan Peninsula of Mexico (especially from Cozumel) and off La Guiara, Venezuela. However, sailfishing is patchy around the Caribbean islands and in the Bahamas.

Atlantic sails are protected in Florida and by the federal billfish management plan. Almost all caught in the US are released. Female sails reach maturity at about 30 to 40lb (13–18kg), and males at about 22lb (10kg). Though their lifespan is relatively short, one tagged sailfish was recaptured after almost 11 years at large.

Pacific sails average twice the size of their Atlantic cousins, but most anglers don't consider them as good a fighting fish on a pound-for-pound basis. Twenty-lb tackle is perfect for them, and nothing larger than 30lb should be used. They move north to the Sea of Cortez (Gulf of California) as waters warm in the spring, but are most abundant further south along the Central American coast, especially off Costa Rica.

Sailfish flesh is of poor quality, though it does make a tasty dish when smoked.

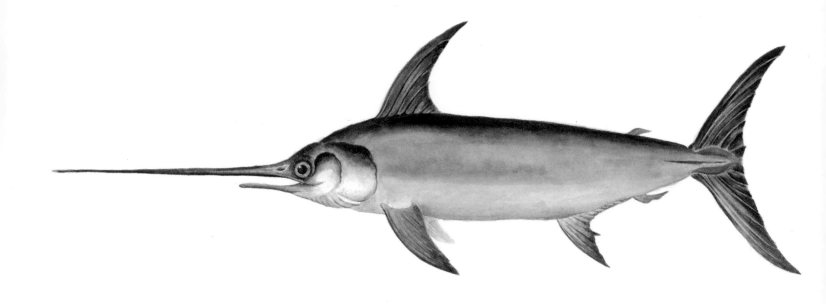

Swordfish

Xiphias gladius

DATA

Habitat: Offshore to oceanic waters.

Habits: All depths.

Range: Worldwide in temperate and tropical seas, and most likely to be encountered from Massachusetts to Florida and off southern California.

Size: Average 100–500lb (45–227kg); but may exceed 2,000lb (908kg)).

IGFA Record: 1,182lb (536.6kg), Chile, 1953.

The swordfish is one of the most elusive prizes in marine angling. That was the case even in the "good old days" of swordfish abundance, when anglers would seek them exclusively on the surface. Unrelenting commercial pressure (except for a brief period when sale was forbidden owing to a scare about mercury content in swordfish) reduced their numbers to such an extent that the surface fishery has become virtually an historic footnote in the Atlantic. However, anglers tried their own version of the longlining technique in the canyons during the late 1970s and caught a great many swordfish while drifting at night with lines set at various depths.

Unfortunately, a steady increase in longlining has reduced the chances of success with even that technique to a very low level. Swordfish longliners have spread over the world just as the whalers did a century earlier, and now find the best swordfishing in such distant areas as the Grand Banks off Newfoundland. Unless the federal government, the fisheries councils, and the industry can get together on a management plan with teeth in it, the long-term prospects for this great fish are dim.

Swordfish are the only member of their family, and cannot be mistaken for any other fish. The sword is long and flat, and the fish lacks pelvic fins. The dorsal fin is high and sickle-shaped, making it very easy to identify a swordfish when he's tailing. Swordfish tend to feed deep at night and sun themselves during the day. They often lie motionless at the surface and are very easy to approach, making them an ideal target for harpooners. Vast numbers have been caught in that fashion with the aid of spotter planes, but longlining at night has proven so effective that there just aren't enough left in reasonably near-shore areas of the north Atlantic to justify the previous level of harpooning – though that technique remains dominant in southern California.

Sportfishers always had a hard time hooking those "sleeping" fish. The technique involved trolling a bait in front of the swordfish and then letting it sink there. Only about one in ten swordfish would hit the bait, and most of those were lost because the hook would tear out of the mouth in the course of the fight. This was the main reason for using two-hook rigs.

Swordfish are normally sought with 80 or 130-lb tackle, though the average size along the Atlantic coast has declined with intense exploitation to the point where most of those caught are merely "pups". A few swords in the 100–300lb (45–136kg) class are still boated each year by fishing canyon waters at night, but the great night Gulf Stream fishery off south-east Florida has virtually died out. For sportsfishers seeking swordfish on the surface, the southern California fishery is by far the best bet. The very largest swordfish tend to come from cooler waters off Peru, Chile and the Maritime Provinces of Canada. The long-standing all-tackle world record is a 1,182-pounder (536.6kg) caught on May 7, 1953 off Iquique, Chile, by Lou Marron.

The biggest problem for the swordfish is the fine quality of its flesh, which brings a premium price throughout the world. As a result, it will probably always be one of the most difficult species for the angler to encounter – much less capture!

THE TUNA TRIBE
Thunnini

The tuna tribe belongs to the mackerel family Scombridae and subfamily Scombrinae – along with the bonitos, Spanish mackerels and mackerels. With their streamlined bodies, tunas provide everything one can ask of a great game fish in terms of speed, power, and endurance. Their only deficit is the failure to jump when hooked, though they frequently clear the water in arching leaps to bounce upon prey. For some anglers, tunas in the largest sizes are just too good a game fish – so powerful that the fish often wins the fight.

Tunas have an advantage over most other fish in that they are not strictly cold-blooded. Their body temperature has been recorded as much as 18°F (8°C) higher than the temperature of the surrounding waters. Dr Frank Cary, of the Woods Hole Oceanographic Institute in Massachusetts, estimates that such a rise in body temperature effectively triples the muscle power of the fish.

Almost all tunas are subject to intense commercial exploitation. In just a couple of years in the 1960s, east coast bluefin stocks had been reduced to about 10 per cent of what they had been. The bluefin stocks were in big trouble before the federal government was prodded into action by Frank Mather of Woods Hole Oceanographic Institute.

ABOVE: Fishermen at Prince Edward Island used to think giant tunas were sharks, but now these valuable fish are treasured.

LEFT: A bluefin tuna, displaying the tail shape typical of all tunas.

Though tunas weren't included in the Magnuson Act which established the US 200-mile (322km) fisheries jurisdiction in 1976, the State Department eventually negotiated an agreement with the Japanese and Canadians which eliminated Japanese longlining in the Gulf of Mexico and placed quotas on the bluefin catches which could be made each year by the US, Japan, and Canada. This system is reviewed each year by the International Commission for the Conservation of Atlantic Tunas (ICCAT).

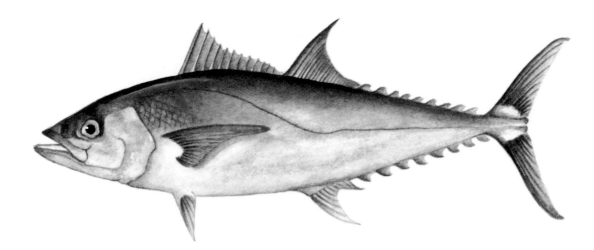

Bluefin Tuna

Thunnus thynnus

The bluefin probably deserves the title of "greatest fighting fish in the world", though it certainly isn't the most spectacular. Catching bluefins requires lots of hard work on the part of the angler, as the fish will fight until overwhelmed. This is, by far, the largest of the tunas – with the all-tackle world record being a 1,496lb (679kg) giant caught at Auld's Cove, near Canso Causeway, Nova Scotia on October 26, 1979 by Ken Fraser.

This highly migratory species has been known to cross the Atlantic Ocean, but American and European stocks seem to be basically separate. American giants migrate south in the fall before wintering and spawning in the Gulf of Mexico. They then move north in the spring on the east side of the Gulf Stream (providing a fishery in May off Bimini and Cat Cay, Bahamas) before heading inshore in northern waters from New Jersey to the Canadian Maritime Provinces and Newfoundland.

Unlike the other large tunas, bluefins are basically an inshore fish in the summer – often being found relatively close to shore and in fairly shallow waters. Several decades ago they were frequently seen chasing schools of mossbunkers at the mouth of Narragansett Bay, Rhode Island – and they still may be spotted at times in the shallows of Cape Cod Bay.

School and medium bluefins move inshore above Cape Hatteras in the spring and work their way up the coast to waters offshore of Cape Cod. However, the school fish rarely migrate north of there – and

DATA

Habitat: Inshore to offshore waters.

Habits: All depths.

Range: Gulf of Mexico through the North Atlantic. Southern California.

Size: School (10–135lb/4.5–61kg), mediums (135–310lb/61–141kg), giants (310lb/141kg to possibly over 2,000lb/907kg).

World Record: 1,496lb (679kg), Nova Scotia, 1979.

mediums do so only in some years. Throughout the summer and fall, the fishery for school and medium bluefins is concentrated from northern New Jersey to Block Island. These immature fish then move to the east during the fall to find comfortable waters for the winter.

Identification of bluefins in smaller sizes can be difficult, particularly after death. Color is a variable, but the pectoral fins are relatively short – extending back only as far as the 11th or 12th spine in the first dorsal fin. The bluefin also has the highest gill raker count in the tribe, with 34 to 43 on the first arch. Both of these characteristics distinguish the bluefin from the bigeye – while another means of telling it apart from a yellowfin is the striated liver with the middle lobe usually the longest.

Bluefins are highly valued as a gourmet food by the Japanese, and that fact has made the pursuit of giants a commercial enterprise even among sportsfishers. Virtually all giants are bought at dockside for prices averaging (in 1990) $5 to $15 a pound (headed and gutted) and ranging as high as $38 a pound.

As a result of the great value placed on the giants, there is little semblence of sportfishing involved in many areas – with tackle much heavier than allowed by the IGFA used in their capture.

Bluefin tuna fishing started in southern California when Dr Charles F Holder boated a 183-pounder (83kg) off Catalina Island on the crude tackle of the time in 1898. A trolling fishery for mediums continued there each summer through World War II, but intensive commercial fishing practically eliminated the Pacific bluefins. Now California anglers catch primarily one-to-two-year-old fish in the 15–30lb (7–14kg) class – and not too many of them. Live bait fishing with very light tackle accounts for most of those line-shy fish. Some giants are taken on rare occasions by commercial fishermen, but the Pacific bluefin doesn't appear to grow much larger than 500lb (227kg).

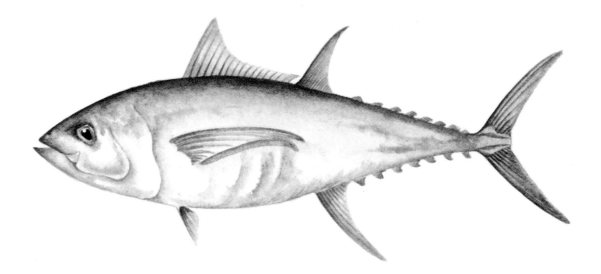

Yellowfin Tuna

Thunnus albacares

DATA

Habitat: Offshore to oceanic waters.

Habits: All depths.

Range: Worldwide in tropical and subtropical waters. In the Atlantic, north to Cape Cod. Also in the Caribbean and Gulf of Mexico. Common off Hawaii, but caught only occasionally as far north as southern California.

Size: Average 50–100lb (23–45kg), grows to at least 400lb (182kg).

World Record: 388¾lb (153.8kg), Mexico, 1977.

Yellowfin tuna are found in many areas where the bluefin is absent because it prefers cooler waters. Yellowfins are also more oceanic than the bluefin, though they do come into shallower waters at times. That was the case for several years in a row off Montauk and Block Island, and the Mud Hole area off northern New Jersey during the mid-1980s. However, most yellowfins are caught from blue waters in, or near, the canyons, and drop-offs of the continental shelf.

Yellowfins seem to prefer water temperatures exceeding 70°F (21°C), though they'll often stay in waters averaging around 60°F (18°C) if there's an abundance of bait – and I saw one caught in Hudson Canyon in mid-November when the surface water was only 58°F (14°C).

There's no way to mistake a yellowfin which develops over-extended second dorsal and anal fins. These beautiful fish used to be called Allisons, and were considered to be a different species. However, scientists now classify them as just a variation of yellowfin. Without those bright yellow, extended fins, the yellowfin (particularly when dead) can be confused with a bluefin or bigeye. It can be distinguished from the former by both the longer pectoral fin (greater than 80 per cent of the head length) and the gill raker count of 27 to 33 (as opposed to 34 to 43). However, the surest feature is the yellowfin's smooth liver – in contrast to the striated livers of the bluefin and bigeye. When alive, yellowfins are without a doubt the most colorful of tunas, with golden-yellow upper sides and yellow fins.

Most yellowfins are caught by trolling, and some of the largest hit high-speed marlin lures off Hawaii. However, the San Diego party boats basically utilize live baits, while dead baits fished in a chum slick with light tackle is the key to great sport with smaller yellowfins on Argus and Challenger Banks off Bermuda. When yellowfins move inshore off New Jersey and New York, they're taken by the same chunking techniques as are bluefins – and those methods also work at night in the canyons during the summer and early fall – before the fish revert to daytime feeding as the waters cool.

Yellowfins are the primary species sought for canning as chunk light tuna. They're excellent when eaten raw or cooked in a variety of ways. However, because their flesh is not as oily as the bluefin's and bigeye's, they aren't nearly as desired by the Japanese – and prices are high only when they are not abundant.

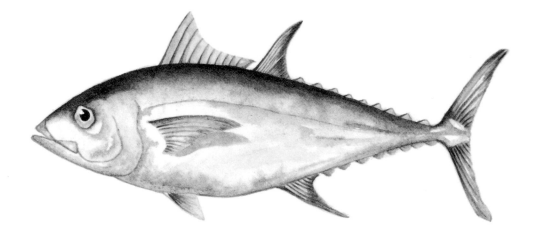

Bigeye Tuna

Thunnus obesus

Bigeyes inhabit warm, temperate, and very deep waters throughout much of the world, and are much more oceanic than the yellow-fin. In the western Atlantic, they're most common in the northern canyons from the Hudson east – though some are caught in the more southerly canyons. A winter commercial trolling fishery has been developed off northern North Carolina. Even in the north, bigeyes rarely stray far inshore of the continental shelf drop-off.

Their very large eye is an indication of a tendency to feed at night. The basic sport-fishing method of high-speed trolling during the day probably only intercepts the relatively few bigeyes who chase bait during their "off-hours". Even when chunking in the canyons at night, anglers usually find that the bigeyes hit deeper lines – and may be feeding below yellowfins which are being hooked just below the surface. Chunking is most effective at night during warm weather, but can be good during the day in the fall.

Live mackerel are used very effectively for bigeyes in daytime fishing at Madeira off northern Africa, but east coast anglers haven't found a consistent source of such baits as yet. Most California bigeyes are caught incidentally while trolling for marlin or live-baiting for albacore and bluefins.

DATA

Habitat: Oceanic waters.

Habits: All depths.

Range: Atlantic coast from North Carolina to Cape Cod – primarily in the canyons. Pacific coast from Washington to Peru, but not abundant in US waters. Also taken off Hawaii.

Size: Atlantic average 100–200lb (45–90kg); up to 400lb (182kg). California average 50–100lb (23–45kg).

RIGHT: A giant bluefin tuna caught on Stellwagen Bank, Massachusetts.

The chunky bigeye can be mistaken for a yellowfin in the smaller sizes, though its eye is bigger and the pectoral fin is even longer. The gill raker count, at 25 to 29, is similar – but the striated liver provides sure identification.

Bigeyes are rated just below giant bluefins as a fresh fish by the Japanese, and the price for similarly sized bigeyes is almost always much higher than for bluefins.

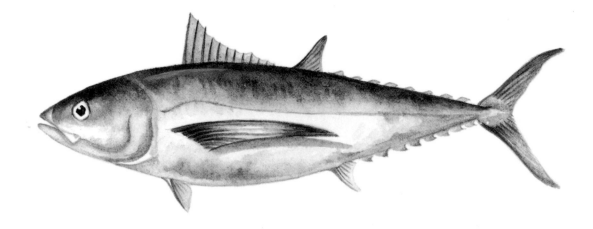

Albacore

Thunnus alalunga

This oceanic tuna is also referred to as "longfin" – an apt description since the very long pectoral fins (which reach to beyond the anal fin) are a dead giveaway as to the species. Albacore are relatively bland in color as compared to the outer oceanic tunas, and their body shape is also slimmer. Only the juveniles can be confused with other tunas, but even they are distinguished by the lack of any spots or stripes on the lower flanks and belly, and a thin, white margin on the tail fin.

Whereas most California albacore are line-shy fish caught on light lines with small live baits (normally anchovies) after the schools are first located by trolling, the Atlantic albacore are usually among the least fussy of tunas. Great numbers are caught in the canyons from late-August well into the fall. Trolling feathers and other relatively small lures is most effective at first, but daytime chunking often becomes so productive in October and November that party boats are able to load up with longfins averaging 30 to 50lb (14–23kg) – and ranging up to 70lb (32kg) or more. This fishing may still be very good even with water temperatures in the 55–60°F range (13–16°C). Pacific albacore are most frequently caught in 60–66°F (16–19°C) waters.

Though little is known about the migrations of albacore in the Atlantic, the trans-Pacific path has been well documented. To illustrate the difficulty involved in keeping

DATA

Habitat: Offshore to oceanic waters.

Habits: Mid to surface feeder.

Range: Worldwide in tropical, subtropical, and temperate oceanic waters except for the tropical Eastern Pacific. In the Western Atlantic, the mid-Atlantic canyons and inshore occasionally from Montauk east. In the Eastern Pacific, from Baja California to south-east Alaska.

Size: Average 25–50lb (11–23kg) (Atlantic), 15–30lb (7–14kg) (California). Maximum over 90lb (41kg).

up with these fish, one tagged off California was recovered off Japan 294 days later – a distance of 5,000 miles (8,045km), which averages out to over 17 miles (27km) a day if the fish was swimming in a straight line.

Albacore have lighter meat than other tunas, and are the only member of the family which can be marketed as premium "white-meat tuna". They are an excellent eating fish, but the lack of oiliness which makes them more desirable to the American palate also reduces their value to the Japanese.

BELOW: **Albacore can be recognized immediately by their long pectoral fins.**

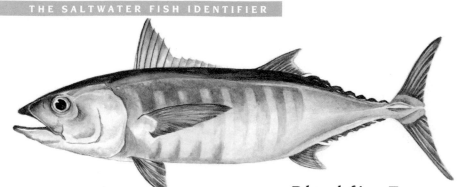

Blackfin Tuna

Thunnus atlanticus

The blackfin is the smallest of the *Thunnus* genus in the Atlantic. This is the common tuna in Florida, and some are caught during the summer north to North Carolina – though only occasionally are a few very small specimens encountered in the canyons further north. Some of the largest blackfins are taken by chumming on Argus and Challenger Banks off Bermuda.

Blackfins are oceanic fish which are most consistently abundant on the humps offshore of the Florida Keys. They are fine game fish on light tackle, and great numbers are trolled there with both balao and small lures. But by far the best method involves the use of live bait, and many Keys skippers bring live wells full of pilchards and chum

---

DATA

Habitat: Offshore to oceanic waters.

Habits: Mid to surface feeder.

Range: Atlantic coast from Florida to North Carolina, including Bermuda, and very rarely to the canyons north of there. Also encountered south to Brazil and in the Caribbean. Common in the western Gulf of Mexico.

Size: Average 5–25lb (2–11kg); up to 50lb (23kg).

---

with them to turn the blackfins on – after which they can be caught on the live baits or tempted with lures and flies retrieved at high speed. Another area in which to seek out record blackfins is around the shrimp boats anchored during the day in the Gulf of Mexico off Key West. Great numbers of blackfins averaging 15 to 25lb (7–11kg) hang around those shrimpers in the spring and will respond immediately when the scrap (crabs and small fish) from night-time shrimping operations is thrown overboard. Fish from that chum will tempt the feeding tuna, as will various jigs, metal lures and plugs.

Though not often mixed with the larger members of the tribe, blackfins can be identified by the uniformly dark finlets (lacking any of the yellow coloration present in other tunas) and the fewest number of gill rakers of any tuna – 19 to 25 on the first arch (15 to 19 on the lower limb).

Blackfins are excellent food fish with relatively light flesh.

The skipjack is instantly recognizable by the unique stripes on its belly plus the absence of any markings on the back. This is a relatively small, but fast-growing species, often found in huge schools which may contain over 50,000 individuals.

Skipjacks grow to 18in (46cm) and achieve maturity within a year, but rarely live longer than seven years. Very large specimens are rare, and the IGFA all-tackle world record of 39lb, 15oz (just under 18kg) from Walker's Cay, Bahamas in 1952 stood until a 40-pounder (18kg) was boated off Mauritius in 1971 (creating an official tie) – and another of 41lb, 15oz (19kg) was also boated off Mauritius in 1985. This fish has been given such misnomers as Arctic bonito and oceanic bonito over the years, but it never approaches the cold waters of the Arctic – and is a member of the tuna tribe, rather than the bonitos.

Though skipjacks are fine fighting fish on appropriate tackle, most are winched in on heavier gear intended for larger species.

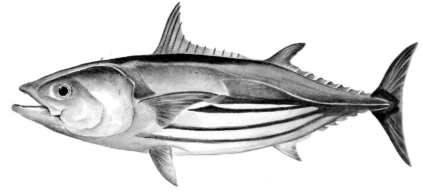

Skipjack Tuna

Euthynnus pelamis

DATA

Habitat: Inshore to oceanic waters.

Habits: Surface feeder.

Range: Worldwide in tropical and subtropical waters. In the Atlantic from Cape Cod to Florida. In the Eastern Pacific from Peru to Vancouver Island, and British Columbia.

Size: Average 3–12lb (1–5kg); up to over 40lb (18kg).

While hardly anyone fishes specifically for skipjacks, they save many a day of summer trolling by keeping the rods bending. Like all the tunas, they are very fast but many are lost owing to hooks pulling out of their soft mouths, which has resulted in the nickname of "mushmouths".

The dark and relatively soft meat of the skipjack isn't highly desired for most uses. However, if bled immediately they are a decent eating fish – and only of slightly lower quality than yellowfins when processed. Purse seiners pursue skipjacks for low-priced canned tuna, but this very prolific species appears to be holding its own.

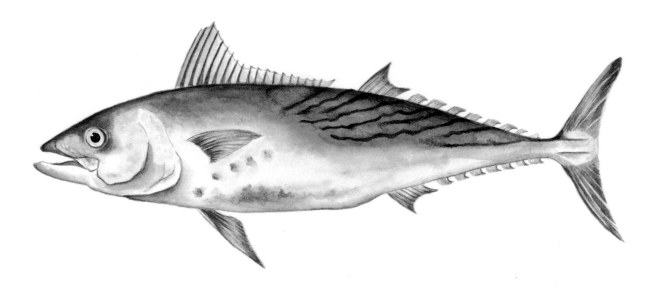

Little Tunny

Euthynnus alletteratus

This great game fish may be the finest fighting and least respected fish in the world. Even among the tunas, it displays unusual speed and endurance – often literally fighting to the death on light tackle. Unfortunately, it is burdened with a poor official name and regional nicknames which confuse it with other species.

The little tunny can be easily recognized by looking for the unique black spots below the pectoral fins plus the wavy, "worm-like" markings on the back. The common name in the north-east is "false albacore", though the little tunny has a very short pectoral fin rather than the long pectoral of the albacore. In the south-east and Gulf of Mexico, the common name is "bonito", which is even less accurate because it refers to another tribe of the family. In Bermuda they're placed even further away from the tunas by being called "mackerel".

Little tunny are prevalent in the Mediterranean as well as both sides of the Atlantic. They are replaced in the Pacific by the very similar black skipjack (E. *lineatus*), which occurs off the eastern Pacific coast from Peru to Baja California, and by the kawakawa (E. *affinis*) from Hawaii through the western Pacific.

The little tunny is the least oceanic of the tunas, and is commonly found right into the surf from mid-summer to early fall from

DATA

Habitat: Surf to offshore waters.

Habits: Surface feeder.

Range: Atlantic, from Cape Cod to Florida and into the Gulf of Mexico.

Size: Average 5–15lb (2–7kg); up to over 35lb (16kg).

Hatteras north to Martha's Vineyard and Nantucket. It generally feeds on small bait fish and can be very difficult to fool with lures. Most are caught by high-speed trolling with feathers, cedar plugs and small metal lures, but the real challenge is involved in casting to them. Light spinning tackle and very small jigs and metal lures should be cast just ahead of the actively feeding fish, and must be retrieved as fast as the handle can be turned in order to fool the sharp-eyed little tunny. They must be tempted to strike by instinct at something flashing by, and will rarely hit once they start following a lure.

Release is the way to go with little tunny, as they have the poorest-quality flesh among the tunas. The dark, coarse, and bloody meat is difficult to work with, though it can be utilized for tuna salad if the fish is bled immediately and the fillet is soaked overnight in refrigerated, salted water before being steamed or boiled.

ABOVE: Little tunny is a terrible name for this great game fish. Look for the spots under the pectoral fin as a clear identification mark.

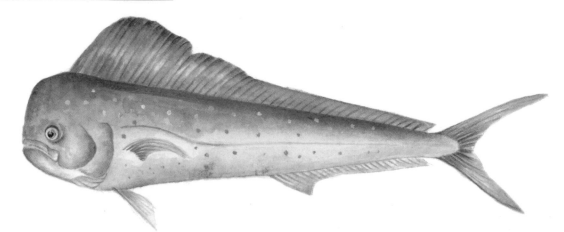

Dolphin

Coryphaena hippurus

The name of one of the most colorful fish in all the oceans creates confusion because it's shared with a family of mammals. Anglers are forever having to assure others that they're not killing "Flipper". Indeed, the confusion caused by the identical names has led many fish markets and restaurants to label the dolphin by its Hawaiian name of mahi-mahi or the Spanish name dorado. The latter is appropriate, as this is truly a golden fish – which also displays many other colors while alive before fading to a uniform dull yellow or silver upon death.

In the water the dolphin usually displays a greenish-blue or yellow appearance, and

---

DATA

Habitat: Offshore to oceanic waters.

Habits: Surface feeder.

Range: Worldwide in tropical and subtropical oceanic waters – off North America from Florida to Cape Cod, Bermuda, Bahamas, Caribbean, and Gulf of Mexico. Also common in the Pacific off Hawaii, but rarely ventures north of Baja California.

Size: Average 1–10lb (0.45–5kg), but common to 40lb (18kg) and may exceed 100lb (45kg).

---

may also show dark vertical bands when excited. The color changes rapidly as the fish dies, and the sides are sprinkled with dark and light spots. The relatively high and continuous dorsal fin and the long anal fin are other identifying factors in a species which can't be mistaken for any other except the only other member of the family – the pompano dolphin (*Coryphaena equisetis*). The latter is a small fish (probably only growing to 5lb/2kg or so) which is probably more oceanic than the dolphin, and can be confused with young females. However, it's much rounder than the slender dolphin, and can be identified by counting more than 240 scales in the lateral line and 56 or more rays in the dorsal fin.

Dolphin are unique in the largely unisex fish kingdom in that males can be visually identified from females in all but the smallest sizes. Males develop a very blunt forehead and, unlike most other species, grow larger than the females.

This species ranks with the great game fish, though big game anglers often shy away from them while in pursuit of billfish. Dolphin are among the fastest fish in the sea, and will attack very large baits and lures. They are also among the fastest-growing of all species, and appear to have a life-cycle lasting only a few years. Very small dolphin (referred to as "chickens") stay in schools and associate with floating debris. As they get larger, they tend to break off into smaller schools or male/female pairs, though the tendency to hang around floating logs, pallets, and fish boxes never leaves them.

Dolphin are most abundant in the spring off south-east Florida and Cape Hatteras, North Carolina. Further north, large dolphin are usually taken in or near the canyons, but schools of chicken dolphin are frequently encountered during late summer within 20 miles (32km) of shore up to Long Island when blue, warm waters move in.

Dolphin eat almost anything found in their environment, and are one of the few fish fast enough to capture flying fish. Anglers usually troll balao or a variety of feathers and high-speed lures in order to tempt them. All sorts of small lures will work, but the retrieve must be fast.

Dolphin are an excellent eating fish with a delicate flesh which must be kept cool. The leathery skin is usually stripped off first before filleting.

ABOVE: The rounded head of this brightly colored dolphin indicates it is a female. The male's head grows more blunt upon maturity.

Wahoo

Acanthocybium solanderi

The wahoo is a member of the mackerel family Scombridae but is included in this section with the billfish and dolphin because it's an oceanic species which is most often caught while seeking the aforementioned fish. In short bursts, the wahoo may well be the fastest of fish – and the name is reputed to have come from the reaction of anglers when one hits and streaks off for the horizon. Fortunately, wahoo usually tire after that first sizzling run, and the fight doesn't last long except on very light tackle.

There is never any question about identification with wahoo. They have long, slender bodies, and the mouth is full of small but very sharp teeth which can slice through a bait or heavy monofilament so quickly that the angler often isn't aware that it has happened. Frequently the line won't even be pulled out of the outrigger pin, and you'll never know that the bait has been sliced in half unless you see the swirl. One of the most spectacular sights in fishing is that of a wahoo making a long, high, arching leap to crash down on a bait. Yet, despite those aerial acrobatics, wahoo don't jump when hooked.

A live wahoo has beautiful black vertical bars on its sides which form unique patterns and immediately distinguish it from its closest cousin, the king mackerel (*Scomberomorus cavalla*). Another unusual feature of the wahoo is that it has no gill rakers.

Wahoo are true oceanic wanderers and do not school in the Atlantic. Thus, catching them is usually a chance situation while trolling for other species with either bait or

DATA

Habitat: Offshore to oceanic waters.

Habits: Mid to surface feeder.

Range: Worldwide in tropical and subtropical oceanic waters, in North America from Florida to Cape Cod, Bermuda, Bahamas, Caribbean, and Gulf of Mexico. Common off Hawaii, but rarely found north of Baja California.

Size: Average 20–60lb (9–27kg); up to 150lb (68kg) or more.

BELOW: The beautiful barred pattern of a live wahoo is one of the great sights in fishing. This one was being released.

high speed lures. However, they are reasonably common at times off south-east Florida, Cape Hatteras, and in the Gulf of Mexico off Louisiana. Large numbers are often encountered in the Bahamas and off Little Cayman in the spring, but the best fishing I ever enjoyed for this species in the Atlantic was on Barracuda Bank off the British Virgin Islands in December.

Though wahoo are surface fish, it's much more effective to troll for them somewhat deeper. The use of wire line or downriggers will greatly increase the catch when wahoo are present.

This is one of the finest eating fish in the world, and so few are captured by commercial techniques that it also constitutes a rather unique meal for the sportfisher.

THE SHARKS

Chondrichthyes

These ancient creatures belong to a class of the cartilaginous fishes. They are basically different from the bony fishes we have discussed so far in that they have cartilaginous skeletons which are more or less calcified but lack true bone. Other unique features of the sharks are five to seven paired gill openings located at least partly on the sides of the head (bony fishes have only one pair of gill openings), and a skin with a sandpapery texture due to being covered with minute tooth-like scales. The body shape is typically fusiform (torpedo-like), except in the case of the flattened angel shark.

Sharks are found in all oceans, and range in size from tiny to huge. Their teeth are a prominent identifying characteristic, and in most species are arranged in up to five rows, so as front teeth fall out others will move forward to replace them. Reproduction in most sharks is also unique, in that it takes place through internal fertilization of the female's eggs via the male's prominent claspers located on the inner edges of the pelvic fins. The young are born alive in most sharks, but relatively few are produced at one time. Thus, the typically long-lived but slow-growing sharks are especially vulnerable to overfishing.

Wherever large-scale commercial shark fisheries have been started, or programs instituted to cut down the numbers of sharks threatening swimmers, their populations have plunged rapidly. A great increase in longlining off the Atlantic coast and the continuing popularity of sportfishing for sharks seems to be putting a dent in the populations of many species. As a result, the fisheries councils and National Marine Fisheries Service (NMFS) are instituting a shark management plan which will relieve some of the pressure on these fish. Overfishing in California has sharply lowered the abundance of thresher sharks, and commercial fishermen are now threatening to do the same thing to mako sharks.

RIGHT: **Although white sharks have been known to attack humans, the species is relatively rare, and casual harpooning is discouraged.**

The largest of all sharks aren't even predators. The whale shark (*Rhincodon typus*) features a unique spotted color pattern and inhabits all tropical oceans. It grows to 50ft (15.2m) or more, but feeds on plankton. In temperate waters, the basking shark (*Cetorhinus maximus*) isn't nearly as colorful, but it grows just about as large and is distinguished by its exceptionally long gill openings. These two largest of all fishes are completely harmless and can be easily approached for a close look.

The tiger shark (*Galeocerdo cuvieri*) is one of the largest and most feared sharks, with a reputation for eating almost anything, including sea birds and all sorts of garbage. It frequents waters of 70°F (21°C) or more worldwide and grows to 30 feet (10m) but

doesn't provide a very spectacular fight. The sand tiger (*Odontaspis taurus*) is in a family of its own, and not closely related to the tiger. It's a sluggish inshore shark (most abundant in Delaware Bay) which is favored by aquariums because of its sedentary nature and impressive set of teeth similar to that of the mako.

Almost all sharks are edible, and a few bring premium prices. However, the presence of urea in the blood creates an unpleasant ammonia odor if the fish aren't quickly bled, cleaned, and iced down. As a general rule, smaller specimens are better eating than the older fish. Shark meat has long been used throughout much of the world, and is rapidly gaining acceptance in North America.

Shortfin Mako Shark

Isurus oxyrinchus

The shortfin mako is a member of the mackerel sharks family Lammidae along with the white and porbeagle. It is one of the great fighting sharks, and is highly prized by anglers because it grows to a large size and often jumps as high as 20ft (6m) when hooked. Like the tunas and the other mackerel sharks, the mako is somewhat warm-blooded. This very fast shark is the only known natural enemy of the swordfish, often sneaking up on a sunning broadbill to bite off its tail before returning to feed on the nearly helpless fish.

Makos are easily identified by the unique long, slender, and curved teeth which protrude from their mouths. While alive they display a beautiful cobalt blue coloration on the back. Like the other mackerel sharks, the mako has a flattened caudal peduncle, nearly symmetrical crescent-shaped tail, streamlined shape, and pointed snout. A very similar deepwater species of the Atlantic and Gulf of Mexico is the longfin mako (*Isurus paucus*), though it's rarely encountered by anglers.

Makos are most commonly sought by sportfishers from Virginia north to Rhode Island, in the Florida Keys and off the California coast (where it's often referred to as bonito shark). Some very large specimens are caught on the Hump off Islamorada, Florida during the spring, and the northern migration occurs primarily from late May

DATA

Habitat: Offshore to oceanic waters.

Habits: Mid to surface feeders.

Range: Worldwide in tropical and temperate seas.

Size: Average 50–200lb (23–91kg); up to perhaps 1,500lb (681kg) or more.

IGFA Record: 1,115lb (506.2kg), Mauritius, 1990.

into mid July – at which time many shark tournaments are conducted. Makos can tolerate water temperatures as low as 57–59°F (around 10°C), but prefer at least 64°F (18°C). They tend to move east as water temperatures rise in midsummer, but return in late summer and early fall. Most of the early sharking areas along the mid-Atlantic

coast are in the 20 to 40 fathom range, but makos often swim within a few miles of shore during the summer in search of their favorite food from spring through fall – bluefish.

The abundance of mako has decreased greatly along the mid-Atlantic coast since longlining has become more common. Mid-Atlantic anglers now release almost all small makos, and many are pushing for a federally mandated 5 or 6ft (around 1.7m) minimum length. However, in California the vast majority of makos caught are quite small. Very large specimens are unusual there, but some of the biggest makos have been recorded in the Pacific off such areas as Hawaii, New Zealand and Australia – though the official all-tackle IGFA world record of 1990 was a 1,115lb (506.2kg) mako from Mauritius in the Indian Ocean.

One of the great mysteries of marine biology is where all the makos come from. Though males mature at less than half that size, it's believed that females aren't mature at less than about 600lb (272kg) – and shark scientist Jack Casey knows of only three pregnant females which have ever been inspected by scientists.

The mako provides the best eating of the sharks, with its meat looking and tasting like swordfish. It doesn't require any of the special handling necessary with other sharks in order to avoid an ammonia smell.

White Shark

Carcharodon carcharias

The white is the shark most often implicated in attacks on humans. However, it is a relatively rare species which is only occasionally hooked on rod and reel. Indeed, there is no place to go specifically to fish for them – though they seem to appear out of nowhere when a dead whale is found floating offshore. Several large specimens have been harpooned around dead whales off the eastern end of Long Island, and Captains Frank Mundus and Donnie Braddick combined to catch a 3,427-pounder (1,556kg) on rod-and-reel when that specimen was found feeding on a dead whale off Montauk in 1986. Unfortunately, the IGFA decided not to accept that largest fish ever taken on rod-and-reel because the whale was serving as chum – and mammals cannot be used for bait or chum under the IGFA's angling rules.

Very few whites are encountered in warm waters but these rare creatures appear to pup off New York Bight, where quite a few juveniles of under 50lb (23kg) have been caught over the years. Large whites seem to prefer mammals over fish, and are often found around seal concentrations off the Maine coast and around San Francisco.

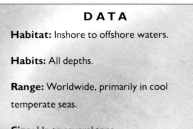

DATA

Habitat: Inshore to offshore waters.

Habits: All depths.

Range: Worldwide, primarily in cool temperate seas.

Size: Up to several tons.

White shark attacks on skin divers and swimmers have been documented in the cool waters of California, but in New Jersey it's necessary to go back to 1916 when three

attacks (two fatal) were attributed to an 8½ft (2.6m) white.

The white is actually a grayish brown above, fading to off-white on the belly. The pectoral fins are black-tipped, but the sure identification of this largest of the mackerel sharks involves the large, triangular teeth with serrated cutting edges. The casual harpooning of these rare fish is now discouraged, since they are a relatively rare species – which isn't surprising in view of the fact that scientists believe maturity isn't achieved until they're at least 15ft (4.6m) long.

BELOW: A 3,427lb (1,556kg) white shark, caught on rod-and-reel off Montauk, NY.

Blue Shark

Prionace glauca

The blue is one of the most abundant sharks in the seas. Though very widespread in the Atlantic, anglers rarely encounter them south of New Jersey since they seem to migrate in deep, cool offshore waters before swinging inshore as they approach New York Bight. A few may wander within 30 miles or so (around 48km) of New Jersey in June, but most are caught 60 miles or more (around 97km) offshore. However, blue sharks move considerably closer to land off eastern Long Island. They were common in Butterfish Hole, 12 miles (19km) south of Montauk Point, into the 1970s – though anglers from that port now more normally have to run 40 miles (64km) offshore in order to encounter large quantities.

Some blue sharks are caught in late May but June is the prime month, and fishing continues east of Block Island throughout the summer. Ideal water temperatures for blues are from about 54°F to about 62°F (12–17°C). However, large blues are often common off eastern Long Island from late August into the fall when the surface waters are still fairly warm. There's relatively little organized sportfishing for blue sharks north of Cape Cod, but the largest American specimens (identical 410-pounders (186kg) caught off Rockport, Massachusetts by

DATA

Habitat: Offshore to oceanic waters.

Habits: Surface feeder.

Range: Worldwide in temperate and tropical oceanic waters – most common off California and from New Jersey to the Canadian Maritime Provinces.

Size: Pacific – average under 100lb (45kg); Atlantic – average 50–200lb (23–91kg), up to over 400lb (182kg).

Richard C Webster in 1960 and Martha C Webster in 1967) have been taken in those colder waters. Slightly larger blues have since been boated in Australia.

Blue sharks are common off California, though most are relatively small, with very few of over 200lb (91kg) having been recorded. However, they've achieved some popularity with fly fishers since they're available in areas reasonably close to shore and will readily hit large flies of many types cast

into the chum slick used to attract them to the boat.

There is no possibility of confusing the blue with any other shark. It is relatively long and skinny, with a long, pointed snout, and floppy, sickle-shaped pectoral fins. The back is light blue, and the belly white. The teeth are nearly triangular and serrated along the edges, but being relatively small they do not make a very impressive jaw mount.

Blues can often be caught in great numbers during their migrations, but are among the poorest fighters of the clan. Light tackle is appropriate, and it's often possible to match the tackle to the fish when they're chummed right to boatside. It is not unusual for skippers to tag as many as 20 to 40 in a day off Montauk in June, and released blues will occasionally come right back to pick up another bait. The NMFS shark-tagging program has amassed a great deal of migratory and growth information on the blue owing to the thousands which are tagged each year by volunteer anglers. While most are recaptured in the same or nearby areas, there have also been many trans-Atlantic and other long-distance recoveries.

Release is by far the best bet with blues, as they are among the poorest eating sharks.

Thresher Shark

Alopias vulpinus

The thresher is among the most distinctive of sharks, with no other identification necessary other than the enormously elongated tail to set it apart from all other sharks except the closely related bigeye thresher (*Alopias superciliosus*). The latter is a deepwater species which is rarely encountered by anglers. It's a slate-gray shark with very large eyes, a longer snout and only 10 or 11 teeth on a side in each of its jaws – as opposed to about 20 in the thresher. The upper lobe of the thresher's tail is about as long as the body, and is used to group schooling fishes in a tight circle during feeding.

Threshers may be the gamest of all sharks, and will put up a good battle even on heavy tackle. The back can be brown, gray, or black with metallic tints. The head and teeth are relatively small, and many large threshers are caught by giant tuna anglers on heavy mono leaders. Threshers appear to mature in a relatively rapid (for sharks) six to seven years, but produce only about four pups. An 18ft (5.5m) female contained four pups averaging 13½lb (6kg) each at lengths of 4 to 4½ft (1.2–1.4m).

Threshers are only abundant off California, where sportfishers have to compete with commercial fishers who capture this highly

---

DATA

Habitat: Offshore to oceanic waters.

Habits: Mid to surface feeder.

Range: Worldwide in warm temperate and subtropical zones. Common from New Jersey to southern New England in the Atlantic and off California in the Pacific.

Size: Average 200–400lb (91–182kg); up to over 800lb (363kg).

---

desired food species for the market. Prime areas for this summer fishery include the San Francisco Bay area, inshore coastal waters between Pt Conception and Pt Hueneme – and Santa Monica Bay, especially around Malibu and Paradise Cove. Threshers average smaller off California than on the east coast, but the largest of all have been caught off New Zealand.

On the east coast, threshers appear to prefer cooler waters than most sharks and are unusual south of New Jersey, where most are caught in June and again during the Mud Hole giant tuna fishery in October.

June and July are also good months for threshers to the east, but this species is not abundant in the Atlantic. Anglers can consider themselves fortunate when they see that long tail thrashing the surface after hooking up.

ABOVE: The extraordinary shape of the hammerhead is a dead give away to the fish's identification.

Hammerhead Sharks

Sphyrnidae family

There are three large hammerheads, all similar in body shape, but each having a distinctive hammer-shaped head. The great hammerhead (*Sphyrna mokarran*) has a flat head with a slight indentation in the middle, while the scalloped hammerhead (*Sphyrna lewini*) features a similar indentation but a rounded hammer, and the smooth hammerhead (*Sphyrna zygaena*) has a rounded head with no indentation. The saw-edged teeth of the great hammerhead are different from the smooth teeth of the scalloped hammerhead and the young smooth hammerhead – though the latter develop serrations as adults.

Hammerheads are usually dull-looking (brown or gray) sharks, and their sluggish appearance as they swim lazily on the surface belies the fact that they are a good game fish and surprisingly fast. In addition, they can also be very fussy eaters. Mid-

> ### DATA
>
> **Habitat:** Offshore to oceanic waters.
>
> **Habits:** Mid to surface feeder.
>
> **Range:** Tropical to warm-temperate seas worldwide.
>
> **Size:** Varies with species.
>
> **IGFA Record:** 991lb (450kg) Florida, USA, 1982.

Atlantic anglers often spot the very tall dorsal fins of hammerheads cruising on the surface in August, but most won't hit a baited hook – and many don't even eat the un-hooked chunks thrown to them. They also often swim in schools during migrations and appear oblivious to what's going on around them; however this is the same fish which will viciously attack large rays, tuna, tarpon, and other species.

The great hammerhead is the largest of the clan, growing to well over 1,000lb (454kg), and prefers tropical offshore waters. It's rarely seen north of Cape Hatteras, but one specimen won a shark contest out of Manasquan Inlet, New Jersey in 1989. The scalloped and smooth hammerheads however commonly move north in the summer to southen New England, and also provide a good deal of sport for southern anglers in waters relatively close to shore. Both are common in the 100–300lb (45–136kg) range, and grow much larger. Unfortunately, the IGFA maintains a world record only for the family, and in 1990 that was still a 991-pounder (450kg) caught off Sarasota, Florida by Allen Ogle in 1982.

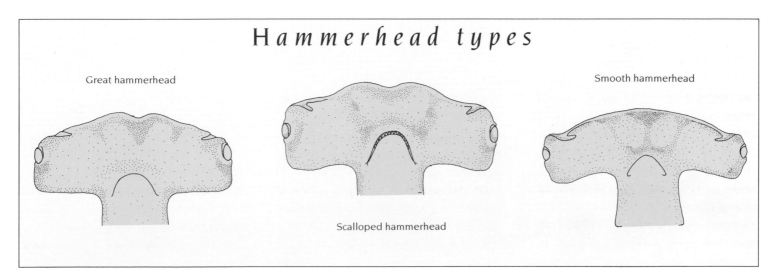

Hammerhead types

Great hammerhead

Smooth hammerhead

Scalloped hammerhead

Sandbar Shark

Carcharhinus milberti

Dusky Shark

Carcharhinus obscurus

These two members of the Requiem shark family are so similar in appearance that it's difficult for all but scientists to tell them apart. Most anglers tend to call those under 100lb (45kg) "browns" (the common name for the sandbar), and the larger specimens "duskys." Both are round-nosed, gray or brownish sharks with a distinct ridge along the back between the dorsal fins. The brown is distinguished from the dusky by a slightly higher dorsal fin (vertical height exceeds 10 per cent of the shark's length) and the placement of that fin further forward in relation to the pectorals.

Browns are the most common shark in the mid-Atlantic, where they enter bays to spawn and also inhabit a wide range of off-shore waters. They're a fine fighting fish but, unfortunately, intensive longlining for both

DATA

Habitat: Inshore to offshore water/bays and surf.

Habits: Bottom feeder.

Range: Atlantic coast from Cape Cod to Florida and into the Gulf of Mexico.

Size: Sandbar – average 30–100lb (14–45kg), up to 200lb (91kg); dusky – to over 600lb (272kg).

the meat and fins is diminishing the abundance of this slow-growing species. Many that were initially tagged in the early days of the NMFS tagging program in the 1960s have been caught after 20 years or more of freedom – with some adults showing surprisingly little growth. However, one I tagged at about 40lb (18kg) off Montauk, NY, in 1976 was taken by a longliner off southern North Carolina just over 13 years later and had grown to 90lb (41kg).

Dusky sharks also are common in inshore waters of the east coast, but larger specimens tend to be found further offshore. Both species are primarily bottom feeders, but can be tempted higher in the water column by a chum slick.

Browns make relatively good eating if they are cleaned promptly.

Bull Shark

Carcharhinus leucas

This may well be the most vicious and dangerous of all sharks. Whereas white sharks rarely interact with man, bulls inhabit shallow coastal waters where visibility is often minimal. They are accustomed to feeding on anything creating a commotion, which could be anything from hooked tarpon to a human being swimming in the surf. Bull sharks are abundant around the river mouths along the Caribbean coast, and the inhabitants in those areas often won't go swimming because of their presence.

> **DATA**
>
> **Habitat:** Inshore waters/surf/rivers.
>
> **Habits:** All depths.
>
> **Range:** Tropical waters, including both brackish and fresh.
>
> **Size:** Average 100–200lb (45–91kg); probably to over 500lb (227kg).

The bull has a short, broadly-rounded snout, a large dorsal fin which is far forward, sub-triangular serrated teeth, and no ridge on the back between the dorsal fins. It's a relatively sluggish fighter which is very common around, and even in, rivers of the south-east and Gulf of Mexico, but rarely strays north of Cape Hatteras.

The "man-eating" Lake Nicaragua shark, the only freshwater shark, is actually now considered by most scientists to be a bull shark which became landlocked.

Atlantic Sharpnose

Scoliodon terraenovae

> **DATA**
>
> **Habitat:** Inshore waters.
>
> **Habits:** All depths.
>
> **Range:** Tropical and subtropical Atlantic and Gulf of Mexico.
>
> **Size:** To about 3ft (1m).

This is a small, shallow-water species within the requiem shark family, but one which is assuming increasing importance in the Gulf of Mexico as a sport fish. It is a species distinguished by its smooth-edged, curved teeth and the presence of well-developed labial furrows around the corners of its mouth. The sharpnose also makes fine eating and is used for food particularly in the Caribbean.

Lemon Shark

Negaprion brevirostris

BELOW: Lemon sharks are active predators on the Florida Keys flats, and will readily hit lures cast to them.

DATA

Habitat: Inshore waters.

Habits: Surface feeder.

Range: Tropical and subtropical waters of the Atlantic, the Gulf of Mexico and the Caribbean.

Size: Average 50–100 lb (23–45kg), up to over 400lb (182kg).

This yellowish-brown, blunt-snouted shark has two triangular dorsal fins which are nearly the same size. Lemons are encountered south of Cape Hatteras, and occur primarily in shallow waters. They are often seen in the clear waters of Florida, Bahamas, and Caribbean island flats. They will respond to flies and plugs drawn right in front of them. Lemon sharks are quite strong, and provide a good battle on light tackle. They are another species responsible for attacks on humans.

Atlantic & Gulf of Mexico Warmwater Inshore Species

This section is devoted to those species most commonly caught from Cape Hatteras south to the Caribbean and into the Gulf of Mexico. Most of them at least occasionally move further north along the Atlantic coast, with many straying as far as Cape Cod during late summer. Several species, including the red drum, croaker, and sheepshead, were apparently relatively common during the last century as far north as New York – but have been very rare there for decades. On the other hand, Spanish mackerel and triggerfish have bcome regular summer visitors to the same areas.

THE MACKEREL FAMILY
Scombridae

The three inshore species of the mackerel tribe within the family Scombridae (which includes the tunas and bonitos) are all slim, streamlined, and exceptionally fast fish. However, their endurance is not nearly as great as that of the tunas. All of these mackerels frequently jump in the course of feeding, but rarely do so when hooked.

With their sharp eyesight, the warmwater mackerels are rarely fooled by slow-moving lures, and anglers should troll at relatively high speeds or cast lures which must be cranked as fast as the handle can be turned. Dead baits can be trolled more slowly, and live baits are the deadliest of all.

All of the mackerels are good eating, though the king mackerel is quite different from the others in both texture and taste. It is a more roundish fish, which can be steaked just like cutting a loaf of bread. The flatter-sided cero and Spanish have oilier flesh and are usually filleted. They are delicious whether baked, broiled, or smoked.

Cero Mackerel

Scomberomorus regalis

This species is far less common than either the king or Spanish mackerels. It's rarely found in the same large schools, and is generally an incidental catch. Ceros also seem to prefer deeper waters and have a much narrower normal range. Most are

DATA

Habitat: Inshore waters.

Habits: Mid to surface feeder.

Range: Western Atlantic Ocean in warm inshore waters.

Size: Average 5–15lb (2–7kg), up to 35lb (16kg).

caught in south-east Florida, and few venture into the northern Gulf of Mexico or above Cape Hatteras. Though frequently confused with Spanish mackerel, there is no problem involved in identifying ceros at a glance. Like the Spanish, they have yellow spots, but the cero's are elongated rather than round and arranged in rows rather than scattered. A prominent straight yellow line shows along the midsection.

King Mackerel

Scomberomorus cavalla

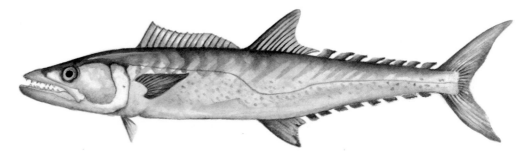

Though the wahoo (belonging to the genus *Acanthocybium*, and described in the previous section) is the largest member of this tribe, the king mackerel is a formidable opponent found much closer to shore. Usually referred to simply as kingfish (not to be confused with the small northern, southern, and Gulf kingfish of the drum family Sciaenidae), this species is one of the most popular and heavily fished sport and commercial fish from North Carolina through Texas. Indeed, that pressure finally caught up with the king mackerel, resulting in a steep decline which led to management plans being adopted by the Gulf and South Atlantic Fishery Management Councils. The introduction of purse seining and massive gill nets quickly put a crimp in a fishery which had traditionally supported both a massive sportfishery and a large fleet of commercial handliners who trolled with

DATA

Habitat: Inshore waters/reefs.

Habits: Mid to surface feeder.

Range: Atlantic Ocean in warm inshore waters.

Size: Average 5–30lb (2–14kg), up to over 100lb (45kg).

wire line and small jigs. Now all segments of the fishery are under severe restrictions, and as a result kingfishing has partially rebounded.

The silvery greenish king mackerel is the least colorful of the tribe, having no yellow spots except when very young. A sure identifying mark is the sharp dip in the lateral line under the second dorsal fin. This migratory inshore species includes an Atlantic component which moves from south-east Florida to summer as far north as Virginia, and a Gulf contingent which becomes the major game fish in Texas waters.

Kingfish favor reefs and other inshore waters, even moving in close enough to the beach to be caught from piers. Jigs and small live baits are effective for smaller schooling kings, while large spoons, trolled balao and live baits of all sorts, are popular for the more solitary large "smokers" – so called because careless anglers "smoke" their thumbs when they try to apply more pressure to a conventional reel spool.

Spanish Mackerel

Scomberomorus maculatus

The Spanish is the smallest and most abundant of the warm-water mackerels, and also tends to enter shallower waters – ranging right into the surf and even into low-salinity bays. It's also found in quantity further north than the other members of the tribe, being common in New York Bight during summers when inshore waters warm well above the 70°F (21°C) mark. Like the king mackerel, it was severely overfished

DATA

Habitat: Inshore waters/surf/bays.

Habits: Surface feeder.

Range: Atlantic coast from Cape Cod to Florida and throughout the Gulf of Mexico.

Size: Average 1–5lb (0.5–2kg), up to 20lb (9kg).

by commercial fishermen and is now regulated by the Gulf and South Atlantic Fishery Management Councils. The comeback of this species is reflected in the significant catches being made at the northern end of its migratory range.

Spanish mackerel are distinguished from the cero by the roundish yellow spots which are not arranged in rows on their silvery skin – and from the king mackeral by both the spots and the lack of a sharp dip in the lateral line below the second dorsal. Most Spanish mackerals found in large schools weigh only a pound or two (about 1kg). They're fine sport on light spinning tackle and will hit small jigs, feathers, and spoons trolled or retrieved at high speed.

THE JACK FAMILY
Carangidae

The jack family may rate right behind the tunas and billfish as great fighters, but most members tend to be downgraded by anglers because they're too tough – without being spectacular. Though the family comprises fast-swimming species, most of which frequently feed on the surface, only the roosterfish (*Nematistius pectoralis*) of the eastern Pacific normally jump when hooked. Many jacks also have dark, strong-tasting meat – and some have been implicated in ciguatera poisoning in areas where that problem is prevalent. Yet among the approximately 140 members of this family found throughout the world is the gourmet's delight – the delicately flavored pompano.

While some jacks have broad bodies and others are slim, all have a forked tail and a rather narrow caudal peduncle, while most have two free spines before the anal fin – though these tend to become overgrown with skin in very large specimens. Many are covered with very small scales, which at the end of the lateral line are enlarged to form a keel. Those large scales, or scutes, are rough to the finger and typify most of these family members.

The carangids most commonly encountered by anglers in the Atlantic and Gulf of Mexico are covered in this section, but the family also includes several other species of interest.

The horse-eye Jack (*Caranx latus*) is similar to the crevalle in size and shape, but lacks the black spot on the pectoral fin. It is most commonly found in the Bahamas, especially at night. The rainbow runner doesn't even look like a jack. It is a streamlined oceanic species, with distinctive blue and yellow stripes, and is found in tropical waters worldwide. A few are caught off Florida, but they are much more abundant off Bermuda and the Pacific coasts of Costa Rica and Panama.

The leatherjacket (*Oligoplites saurus*) is a slim, silvery, warm-water inshore fish with

very sharp dorsal and anal fins which make it risky to handle. The leatherjacket rarely exceeds 12in (30cm) in length, strikes aggressively at small lures, and is partial to dingy waters in estuaries.

The scads are of little angling interest, but can be used as bait for larger species.

All have prominent scutes. The bigeye (*Selar crumenophthalmus*) and rough scads (*Trachurus lathami*) have stocky bodies, with the latter showing enlarged scutes along the entire lateral line. The mackerel (*Decapterus macarellus*) and round scads (*Decapterus punctatus*) are more cigar shaped.

Greater Amberjack

Seriola dumerili

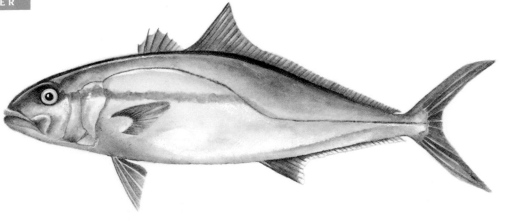

Probably the largest of the jack family, the greater amberjack is simply referred to as amberjack. The Pacific amberjack (*Seriola colburni*) is a similar species found in the eastern Pacific from Baja California south.

Amberjack are easily identified except as juveniles, when they display five body bands. They're a heavy-bodied but relatively slim species (for a jack) with great variation in color, but basically dark above and lighter along the sides. A black stripe from the upper jaw through the eye to the top of the head is often displayed in excited amberjack, and is quite obvious when they're seen in the water. In addition, an amber band may run from the eyes to the tail.

This migratory species is very abundant off south-east Florida in the winter, particularly over deepwater wrecks and humps, and along reefs. During the spring they move north both along the Atlantic coast and into the northern Gulf of Mexico, where they are frequently encountered at oil rigs.

DATA

Habitat: Inshore to offshore waters/ wrecks/reefs.

Habits: Bottom to mid feeder.

Range: Almost worldwide in tropical and warm temperate waters.

Size: Average 30–50lb (14–23kg), up to over 175lb (79kg).

IGFA Record: 155lb 10oz (70.5kg), Bermuda, 1981.

Though common around buoys off the Virginia coast, adult amberjack are uncommon north of Chesapeake Bay, and almost unheard of beyond Cape May, N.J. On the other hand, juvenile amberjack are frequently encountered by bottom fisher-men in New Jersey and New York during late summer.

Until recently, pressure on this species was moderated by the fact that the flesh, while edible, is of relatively low quality – and usually at least partially infested with harmless but unappetizing worms. However, with all other fish worth so much money, great numbers of amberjack are now commercially harvested in Florida and off South Carolina, even though the market price is low. Due to the tendency of this fish to concentrate in specific areas, they are very vulnerable and could easily be fished out of such spots if regulations aren't adopted to protect the resource. It should also be noted that where ciguatera is a problem, this large predator of the reefs should be avoided.

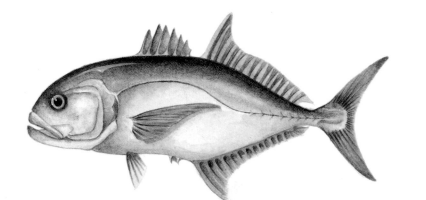

Crevalle Jack

Caranx hippos

The crevalle jack is also known as cavalli or jack crevalle. This broad fish has a blunt forehead and is identified by the black spots on the edge of the gill covers and the

DATA

Habitat: Inshore waters/bays/surf.

Habits: Mid to surface feeder.

Range: Western Atlantic Ocean shores from Cape Cod to Uruguay, including the Gulf of Mexico.

Size: Average 3–15lb (1–7kg), up to over 55lb (25kg).

pectoral fin, and a small circular patch of scales in an otherwise scaleless area between the pelvic fins and the throat.

Crevalle are among the toughest fish in the seas, especially on light tackle. They use their broad bodies to great advantage and circle continuously under the boat, defying the angler to move them upwards.

Crevalle are found in a variety of inshore waters, and will frequently feed in the surf and bays – even running into brackish waters for such favorite prey as mullet. They readily take live baits, trolled strip baits, plugs, spoons, and jigs.

Their meat is dark and relatively strong, and crevalle are rarely appreciated by American anglers who feel they've lost time which could be spent in catching "edible" fish. Crevalle are popular eating fish in tropical countries – although they have been implicated in ciguatera poisoning.

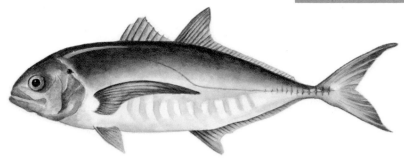

Blue Runner

Caranx crysos

This species, also called hardtail, is very common in warm inshore waters, and is generally regarded by anglers as a bait fish for such species as sailfish, king mackerel, cobia, amberjack, and other large jacks. However, they also put up a lively battle on light tackle. Blue runners are more slender

DATA

Habitat: Inshore waters/bays/surf.

Habits: Mid to surface feeder.

Range: Western Atlantic Ocean from Cape Cod to Brazil, including Bermuda, the West Indies, and Gulf of Mexico.

Size: Average 1lb (0.45kg) or less, but up to 7lb (3kg).

in profile and more rounded in body shape than the crevalle and horse-eye. They have a black spot on the edge of the gill cover, and the straight portion of the lateral line is almost twice as long as the curved portion. Blue runners will readily hit tiny jigs worked fast, and will take a wide variety of small baits – even including the sand fleas used by surfcasters seeking pompano along Florida's Atlantic coast.

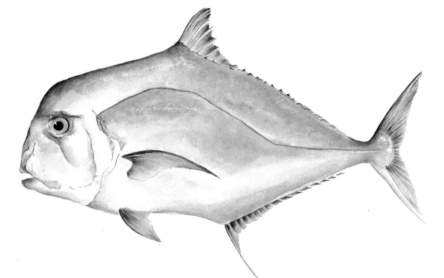

African Pompano

Alectis ciliaris

This is one of the most fascinating marine fishes. While many fish look completely different from the adult form in the tiniest sizes, African pompano weighing several pounds appear to be another species altogether – and were once classified separately as Atlantic threadfin. The juveniles are among the most beautiful of fish, combining the roundish shape of a pompano with four to six elongated, thread-like rays in the front part of the dorsal and anal fins. The first couple of rays may be as long

DATA

Habitat: Inshore waters/reefs.

Habits: Mid to surface feeder.

Range: Almost worldwide in tropical and subtropical waters.

Size: Average 10–30lb (4.5–13.5kg), up to 50lb (23kg).

as four times the length of the fish. Yet, as the fish grows the threads shorten, and may completely disappear in large specimens.

The body shape also changes, becoming more elongated with a very steep forehead. Only the predominantly silver coloration remains to link the juvenile and adult.

African pompano are strong fighters but don't appear to be abundant anywhere. Most of the larger specimens are taken off south-east Florida on live baits fished over reefs for other species. This fish, also formerly known as Cuban jack, is rarely encountered north of Florida in the Atlantic – though some adults are taken in the Gulf of Mexico offshore of Louisiana.

The African pompano makes better eating than the crevalle and horse-eye.

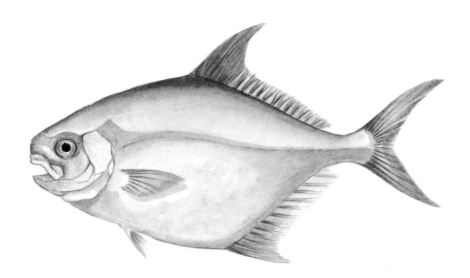

Florida Pompano

Trachinotus carolinus

Invariably referred to simply as pompano, this roundish, golden-hued, shallow-water species carries the Florida before its official name to separate it from two Pacific pompanos, which rarely stray north to California, and the palometa (*Trachinotus goodei*). The latter is also known as the long finned pompano, and is easily distinguished by the four to five narrow vertical bars on the sides, and the very long dorsal and anal fins. The palometa is a small species which appears to be rare in American continental waters, but is common in Bermuda and the Virgin Islands.

Pompano are fine game fish. Though relatively small, they provide great sport when hooked on light tackle. They'll frequently hit small jigs, but most angling catches are made by those fishing with sand fleas in the surf of south-east Florida from October to May. Unfortunately, long, heavy surf rods are required in order to make long casts to the rough bottoms favored by the silver-sided pompano. Prime winter surf areas are from Palm Beach to Hobe Sound, and pompano are also often caught inside the inlets. During the summer, Sebastian is a focal point of Florida pompano fishing, and clams are favored for bait in that area. Pompano range well north in the summer, and are often fairly abundant at Cape Hatteras. However, very few stray any further north. The Gulf of Mexico also gets a shot at pompano in the surf during the summer, and many are caught during the winter at oil rigs off the Louisiana coast.

DATA

Habitat: Surf/flats.

Habits: Bottom feeder.

Range: North Carolina to Florida and the Gulf of Mexico.

Size: Average 1–2 2lb (0.45–1kg), up to over 8lb (3.5kg).

Unfortunately, the price on the head of this fish is a constant threat to its survival. Formerly abundant populations in many areas have been depleted by gillnetting, and prospects for the future are not good unless regulations are imposed.

Pompano are noted as a high-priced species favored by the famous chefs of New Orleans. Pompano en papilote (cooked in buttered white butcher's paper to trap the steam and juices inside) was probably the best-known fish speciality from that city until blackened redfish was popularized.

BELOW: Pompano are members of the jack family and have the typical falcate (sickle-shaped) caudal fin.

Permit

Trachinotus falcatus

DATA

Habitat: Inshore waters/flats/wrecks.

Habits: Bottom feeder.

Range: Florida, Bahamas, Mexico, and some Caribbean islands.

Size: Average 5–25lb (2–11kg), up to 60lb (27kg).

Though generally silvery, permit can vary greatly in color. There's no problem in identifying adults, but the young can be confused with the pompano. However, the permit's body is deeper and may have a circular black area on the side behind the base of the pectoral fin. For definite identification count the soft rays of the anal and second dorsal fins. Both the pompano and permit have three spines in the anal fin, with the first two detached. However, the pompano has 20–23 soft rays while the permit has only 16–19. Both have one spine on the second dorsal, but the pompano has 22–27 soft rays and the permit 17–21.

This is one of the world's great game fish. Not only a fine fighter, the permit is also a great challenge when encountered on the flats. Guides pole anglers over the deeper flats where permit averaging 12–25lb (5–11kg) are encountered singly or in small groups. Small live crabs are by far the best bait, and they must be cast ahead of the fish so the crab can be retrieved in front of the permit as it swims by. The battle on light spinning tackle can go on for an hour or more before the exhausted fish is netted – and usually released.

Permit are a much easier target when they gather in schools over wrecks. On one occasion I caught them one after another on bonefish jigs, but the best bet is still live crabs. However, when Key West guides chum over Gulf of Mexico wrecks with shrimp boat "trash" (unwanted fish and crabs), permit will eat the dead crabs readily. The same technique is used to catch many large permit in Key West Harbor during the course of tarpon fishing.

Permit are also encountered during the spring and summer on wrecks further north in the Gulf, particularly off Marco – but are unusual in the northern Gulf. Along the Atlantic coast, few permit stray above the Florida Keys, though some are caught by accident from the surf and piers of southeast Florida. The most consistent flats permit fishing in the Keys occurs off Key West and at the remote Marquesas. Permit are found in some portions of the Bahamas, but aren't abundant there. A few have been spotted at Los Rocques off the Venezuelan coast, and large numbers of small to medium permit are caught on the Yucatan Peninsula of Mexico.

Though not usually regarded as a food fish, permit are comparable to pompano in the smaller sizes. A 12-pounder (5.5kg) I jigged on a wreck off Marco may have been the best-eating fish I've ever had, but the largest specimens are reputed to be somewhat coarse.

Lookdown

Selene vomer

DATA

Habitat: Bays.

Habits: Mid to surface feeder.

Range: Tropical and subtropical waters on both sides of the Atlantic.

Size: Average ½–1lb (0.2–0.4kg), up to 3lb (1.3kg).

This iridescent silvery fish is characterized by an extremely compressed body and a very high blunt head. The dorsal and anal fin lobes are very long. The closely related Atlantic moonfish (*Selene setapinnas*) has only a moderately high head profile and short dorsal and anal fin lobes. These fish are basically nocturnal and are commonly encountered around lighted docks and bridges in south-east Florida. They'll readily hit tiny jigs fished on very light line.

Despite their small size, they are an excellent pan fish.

THE DRUM FAMILY
Sciaenidae

This large family of inshore species is characterized by their ability to make noises, which is accomplished by the vibration of muscles in the swim bladder – with the bladder acting as a sound box to magnify the drumming or croaking. However, sciaenids without swim bladders also create noise by grinding their teeth together. Scientists believe that noise-making has a function in the reproductive process, though in some species only the male is capable of producing noises.

The lateral line of sciaenids continues to the tip of the caudal fin, which is usually rounded or pointed. The mouth is set low on the head of most species. There are over 200 species of drums throughout the world, and almost all favor the shallow waters of estuaries, and some can even adapt to fresh waters. One family member, the Atlantic croaker (*Micropogon undulatus*) is a popular food fish, averaging ½–1½lb (200–600g). It is common in Chesapeake Bay and also found south to northern Florida and in the Gulf of Mexico. Croakers have a vertical pattern of uninterrupted narrow dark lines on their backs, and a tiny barbel along the inner edge of the lower jaw.

Most of the members of this temperate- and tropical-waters family, which are of prime interest to anglers, will be covered here. However there are a few Pacific members which are profiled in the "Pacific inshore" section, and the weakfish will be covered with the Atlantic coolwater species, though it is also common south of Virginia.

This is the most highly regarded game fish of the family. There is no mistaking a red drum for any other fish. They have a unique copper coloration and there is always at least one black spot about the size of an eye at the base of the caudal fin – while some individuals may have several spread along their body. The small fish, often called puppy drum, readily strike jigs and small spoons, and are one of the most important inshore game fish in the Gulf of Mexico. They inhabit all shallow waters, and can tolerate fresh water to such a degree that several states are trying to adapt them to lakes warmed by power plants or with only slightly saline water.

Large red drum, often referred to as bull reds (though most are actually females), are a prize sought after by many anglers. The early spring and fall fisheries on North Carolina's Outer Banks are famed for producing the biggest red drum of all, including Dave Deuel's IGFA all-tackle record of 94lb 2oz (42.7kg) taken from the surf at

Red Drum

Sciaenops ocellatus

DATA

Habitat: Surf/bays/rivers.

Habits: All depths.

Range: Atlantic coast from Virginia south, plus the Gulf of Mexico.

Size: Average 5–50lb (2–20kg), up to 100lb (45kg).

Avon on November 7, 1984. Most of the red drum caught from the Outer Banks surf and piers are in the 30–50lb (14–23kg) class, but the most consistent way to catch trophy red drum is from charter boats anchored on the dangerous bars of Hatteras and Ocracoke Inlets at night. Some large red drum are also caught during the spring and summer within Pamlico Sound, both on the bars and from the marsh banks.

Red drum, with their underslung mouth, look like bottom feeders. Indeed, most large specimens are caught on dead baits fished on the bottom. However, there are times when schools can be spotted on the surface beyond the outer bars of the surf or in Pamlico Sound – giving anglers an opportunity to cast lures (usually heavy metal jigs) to them. Quite a few red drum are caught at the mouth of Chesapeake Bay and from the Virginia portion of the Delmarva Peninsula.

In recent years the red drum has assumed the role of a prime eating fish. Known as redfish to the south, the red drum has long been regarded as a fine food fish in the smaller sizes. However, specimens over about 15lb were regarded as being too coarse – and were usually released or given to those who couldn't afford any better. As a result, there was little commercial pressure on the spawning population. All that changed when blackened redfish became the rage in New Orleans during the 1980s. The huge catches of big red drum brought in by netters created a crisis in the fishery. The Federal Government and some States had to step in even before the Gulf and South Atlantic Fishery Management Councils could implement the plans which now severely restrict red drum catches. Redfish have been made a game fish in Texas, and that status should spread to most States in the future.

Black Drum

Pogonias cromis

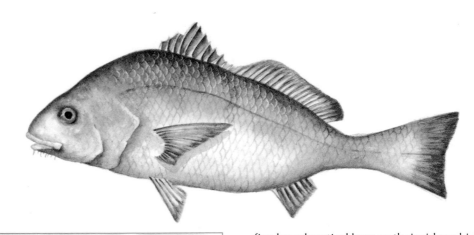

Black drum lack the speed of the red drum, but have the power and endurance to put up a stubborn, if not spectacular battle. Though basically a southern species, the most important sport fisheries for large black drum are located at the mouth of Chesapeake Bay and within Delaware Bay in the spring. Once common in New York, now only stray black drum are taken north of Delaware Bay. Small black drum are commonly hooked by southern bottom anglers and those casting small jigs tipped with shrimp. Very few anglers fish specifically for this species in the southern areas where it's most abundant.

Stockier than red drum, black drum have no spot on the tail. Their underslung mouth is fringed with barbels, and the throat is

DATA

Habitat: Bays/rivers.

Habits: Bottom feeder.

Range: Atlantic Coast from Delaware Bay south, plus the Gulf of Mexico.

Size: Average 5–50lb (2–20kg), up to over 100lb (45kg).

armed with crusher teeth which allow them to feed on shellfish. Juveniles have four or

five broad vertical bars on their sides which fade away completely as they become adults. This species is well known for the drumming noise it produces – a sound which can be heard clearly above the water in shallow waters. Basically a nocturnal fish, large black drum in Delaware Bay are primarily caught with clams fished on the bottom in sloughs.

Black drum are a good eating fish, even in the largest sizes, though cleaning is a job for an expert due to the heavy scales.

Spotted Seatrout

Cynoscion nebulosus

Along with the red drum, this is the prime inshore game fish of the Gulf of Mexico. They populate all of the estuaries and can tolerate water so fresh that some states are experimenting with introducing them into lakes. Though they're very similar to the weakfish, spotted seatrout sport numerous round black spots on their sides, and dorsal and caudal fins. They frequent shallow waters in the Gulf year-round, and are particularly vulnerable to winter kill-offs when temperatures plunge. Commercial fishing

DATA

Habitat: Bays/rivers/surf.

Habits: All depths.

Range: Atlantic coast from Virginia south, plus the Gulf of Mexico.

Size: Average 1–6lb (0.45–3kg), up to 20lb (9kg).

and habitat loss has also put a dent in both the population and the abundance of large specimens. The Indian River in Florida was once famed for its "gator trout" of over 10lb (4.5kg), but such specimens are now rare. Texas has made this species a game fish·

Spotted seatrout are active shallow-water predators and will hit a wide variety of lures and live baits. Two similar species are commonly taken by Gulf anglers. The sand seatrout (*Cynoscion arenarius*) is also called sand trout and white trout. It's an inshore fish which is found only in the Gulf. The sand seatrout lacks spots and may show large, irregular dark blotches on the upper body when viewed from above. The average sand seatrout weighs less than a pound (0.45kg), and they don't grow much larger than 16in (40cm). However, sand seatrout are important pan fish in Texas – where they provide lots of action for pier fishermen in the winter. The silver seatrout (*Cynoscion nothus*) is an even smaller unspotted seatrout which can be distinguished from the sand seatrout by having only 8–9 soft rays in the anal fin as compared to the sand's 10–11 rays. The silver seatrout frequents ocean and Gulf waters, only coming into bays during the cool-weather months.

All seatrout are good eating fish but have soft flesh which spoils quickly and doesn't freeze very well.

Spot

Leiostomus xanthurus

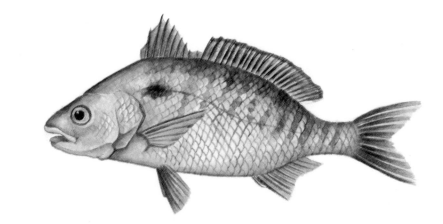

Though a relatively tiny species, the spot is of great importance as a pan fish in Chesapeake Bay and along the coast south of there. It's quickly identified by the distinct brownish spot on the shoulder plus 12–15 yellowish bars on the sides. The male spot makes a drumming sound. Spot are cyclical, and often available in great numbers. Some years they're found in good quantity to the north, being quite common during late summer in the bays and rivers of New York and New Jersey. Around New York Harbor they used to be referred to as Lafayettes, since spot were plentiful during the year that the French

DATA

Habitat: Bays/rivers.

Habits: Bottom feeder.

Range: Atlantic coast from Cape Cod to Florida, plus Gulf of Mexico.

Size: Average under ½lb (0.22kg), up to 2lb (1kg).

hero of the American Revolution arrived. Since it takes on a golden hue at spawning time, the spot may also be mistakingly referred to as "golden croaker." Spot are pursued by many game fish, and are a favorite live bait for weakfish in the fall from New Jersey to the Delmarva Peninsula.

Cobia

Rachycentron canadum

The sole representative of its family, the cobia is often mistaken in the water for a shark, though in shape it's more like a giant remora (shark sucker) – featuring a long, broad, depressed head, but without the suction pad. Cobia are colored dark brown on the upper portion of the body, and a black stripe extends from the snout to the base of the caudal fin. The unique first dorsal consists of 8–10 short, depressible spines which are not connected by a membrane.

Cobia are common in Chesapeake Bay and all along the coast, and also throughout the Gulf of Mexico, but only a few strays are

DATA

Habitat: Inshore waters/bays/flats.

Habits: Surface feeder.

Range: Almost worldwide in tropical and warm temperature waters.

Size: Average 10–50lb (4.5–20kg), up to about 150lb (68kg).

caught during the summer north to New York. In the Gulf they're called ling or lemonfish, and other names applied to this odd-looking species include crabeater, black salmon, black kingfish, cabio and sergeant fish.

Cobia are highly migratory, and like to hang around obstructions or floating objects. Look for them over wrecks and around buoys, channel markers, bridges

and oil rigs. In the course of fishing, one may even slide in under your boat. Guides in both the Keys and along Florida's west coast make a specialty of fishing migrating cobia in the spring by spotting large rays and casting lures or live baits to the cobia swimming underneath them. These fish will hit almost any lure or bait at times, but will also refuse everything on other occasions. In Chesapeake Bay, live baits, such as eels, are the best bet during the summer run – but in North Carolina's Pamlico Sound anglers do very well by simply fishing a dead bait on bottom in the channels. The best fishing of all may occur when cobia gather over wrecks in 60–80ft (18–24m) of water in the Gulf of Mexico. On one occasion, I fished a wreck off Key West on a flat calm day when the cobia rose up to greet us and stayed around the boat all day waiting to be caught and released on everything from flies to plugs and jigs. Anglers must be cautious with these fish, as they rarely are exhausted when captured and can create havoc when swung aboard on a gaff.

Cobia are one of the best eating fish in the seas, and their harvest is now strictly regulated by a South Atlantic Fishery Management Council plan.

Tarpon

Megalops atlanticus

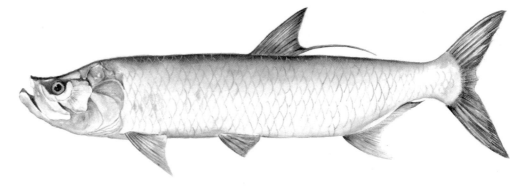

D A T A

Habitat: Inshore waters/bays/flats.

Habits: Surface feeder.

Range: Both sides of the Atlantic Ocean in tropical and subtropical waters.

Size: Average 5–100lb (2–45kg), up to 300lb (136kg).

This herring-like fish is the giant of the small Elopidae family, and has a unique appearance and shape which makes it impossible to confuse with any other species. The silver king has giant armor-like scales (which can be made into art objects), on its almost vertical sides, an underslung mouth, and a last ray in the dorsal fin which is extended into a long filament. One of the largest fish to be found in the inshore waters of North America, the tarpon starts life as an eel-like larvae and take 6 to 7 years before reaching maturity at about 4ft (1.2m). This ancient species has the unique ability to roll on the surface and gulp air directly into its air bladder, making it possible for them to live even in oxygen-depleted stagnant waters. They can also adapt to brackish and fresh waters.

Tarpon are migratory fish, but practically the entire catch comes from the State of Florida. Some are caught along the Atlantic coast from Georgia to Virginia each summer, though only a few ever stray north of the Virginia barrier islands. They were once very common in Texas, particularly at Port Aransas, but now are much harder to come by in the northern Gulf. A northerly migration takes place along both coasts of Florida in the spring, but tarpon can be caught in the winter around Key West – while others never leave the warm water outlet of the Fort Lauderdale power plant. Tarpon of 100lb (45kg) or more are fairly common throughout their range, though the biggest concentration of super-large silver kings appears to be located on the central Gulf coast around Homasassa.

Tarpon of all sizes will hit a wide range of live and dead baits plus lures. As a general rule, the lures should have relatively little action (darters, jigs and flies are the usual choices) and must be drawn slowly across the path of these fish.

Though one of the world's finest fighting fish, the tarpon rates right at the bottom as an eating fish. Fortunately, there's no commercial pressure on it – and Florida not only protects the tarpon as a game fish but even prohibits retention of them without a $50 permit for each capture. As a result, virtually all are released. The only problem is the loss of mangrove habitat for the developing juveniles, which are spawned offshore but grow up in the shallows.

Ladyfish

Elops saurus

D A T A

Habitat: Bays.

Habits: Surface feeder.

Range: Atlantic, Indian and Western Pacific oceans.

Size: Average 1–3lb (0.45–1.5kg), up to about 10–15lb (4.5–7kg).

This only close relative to the tarpon normally taken in North America used to be known by the complete misnomer "tenpounder." Though Migdalski and Fichter in their book *The Fresh & Salt Water Fishes of the World* (Alfred A Knopf, NY 1976) claim a maximum size of 3ft (1m) and 15lb (6.8kg), I can't find an actual record of even a 10-pounder (4.5kg). While serving at the US Naval Station in Trinidad, West Indies around 1960, I caught ladyfish up to 6lb (2.7kg) from the piers at night, but such specimens are very rare in Florida – where great numbers of 1–2lb (0.45–1kg) ladyfish are caught by anglers casting jigs and small plugs for other species.

Ladyfish are great sport on light tackle, hitting hard and jumping constantly. Ladyfish are slimmer than tarpon, have very small silvery scales, and lack the filament on the dorsal fin.

Bonefish

Albula vulpes

The "gray ghost of the flats" was extolled early in the century by Zane Gray as one of the greatest game fish, and that designation is heartily accepted by all who fish for it. Though they are sometimes caught "blind" casting jigs or chumming in channels (in Bermuda the primary method is bottom fishing with worms), most bonefish are taken by sight casting on the flats of the Florida Keys, the Bahamas, and many Caribbean islands and shorelines. Bonefish are very spooky as they feed in only a foot or two (about 50cm) of water, and are often spotted when their tails pop out of the water as they root in the bottom for crabs, shrimp, and worms. Guides pole anglers with light spinning tackle or fly rods to within casting distance, and a shrimp, tiny bonefish jig or

---

DATA

Habitat: Flats.

Habits: Bottom feeder.

Range: Tropical waters worldwide.

Size: Average 3–8lb (1–3.5kg), up to 20lb (9kg).

---

fly, must be placed ahead of the fish without spooking it but close enough to be noticed on the slow retrieve. When hooked, the bonefish may run off a hundred yards of light mono seeking the security of deeper water, and several other runs will follow

until the fish is exhausted and ready to be released. Wading the flats is even more exciting, and bonefish can usually be approached very closely by careful anglers.

Bonefish are primitive bony fish, and share the eel-like larval stage with the tarpon and ladyfish – which also belongs to the order Elopiformes – though the bonefish is the only living member of the family Albulidae. It's distinguished by its silvery body with dark longitudinal stripes on the back, plus a sloping forehead and small subterminal mouth.

Though Americans generally regard them as inedible, bonefish are consumed in most other countries and are actually very good eating once the problem with bones is overcome.

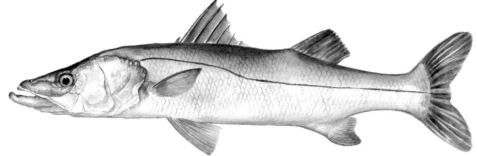

Snook

Centropomus undecimalis

There are actually four species of snook in Florida, but the others are very small fish which are rarely distinguished from juvenile snook. Snook have relatively slender, silvery bodies with a bold, black lateral line which runs right through the caudal fin. Anglers should be aware of the sharp pre-operculum edge which can slice a hand if inserted under the gill cover.

This great game fish of the shallows is caught in a variety of habitats, but is most at home in mangrove areas and around bridges where it can cut an angler's line in a

---

DATA

Habitat: Bays/surf/rivers.

Habits: All depths.

Range: Atlantic coast from Florida south to Brazil, plus Gulf of Mexico and many Caribbean islands and shorelines.

Size: Average 3–20lb (1.3–9kg), up to over 50lb (20kg).

---

flash if the fish isn't powered out of the cover as soon as it's hooked. On the southeast coast of Florida, snook are taken in large numbers with live baits, plugs, and jigs in the inlets, especially at night. Some are even caught from ocean piers, but they rarely move much beyond the surf line. Not only can snook tolerate brackish river waters, but they also readily adapt to fresh waters. Snook are uncommon north of Florida on the Atlantic coast, and in the Gulf are caught primarily south of the Florida Panhandle, and from Galveston, Texas to the south.

Snook are one of the great eating fish of the world, but they've received protection as game fish in Florida. However, they are very vulnerable to winter cold snaps which quickly drive water temperatures down and their abundance has been diminished by the loss of juvenile habitat owing to wetlands development.

Great Barracuda

Sphyraena barracuda

This fearsome-looking species poses no significant danger to man. Though they readily chop other fish in half, cuda avoid anything larger than themselves. The only likelihood of being bitten by one underwater is under murky conditions when a cuda might strike at the flash of a bright object. Unfortunately, owing to their fierce reputation, barracuda were regarded as trash fish in Florida until recent years – and they aren't nearly as abundant now that they're valued as fine game fish.

Barracuda are good fighting fish wherever caught, but they are at their finest when hooked on light tackle in the shallow waters of the Florida Keys flats, where they are abundant during the winter months. Cuda provide slashing strikes on tube lures skittered across the surface and make long, fast runs spiced with impressive leaps. Also look for large quantities of barracuda around the various navigational structures on the reef. Trolling with lures and live or dead baits is the best means of locating solitary cuda on the reefs and over grass patches inside the reef. Small barracuda are readily available to those wading from shore along the Atlantic side of the Keys, and I've had good luck catching them on fast-retrieved small spoons and tubes.

Barracuda migrate north along the Atlantic coast, and are fairly abundant up to North Carolina in the summer – though they are unusual north of there. They are found throughout the Gulf of Mexico in the summer, but are most common at offshore oil rigs. The Bahamas play host to vast numbers of barracuda, and they are also common around all the Caribbean islands and coastlines.

DATA

Habitat: Inshore waters/reefs/flats.

Habits: Surface feeder.

Range: Tropical seas worldwide except for the eastern Pacific.

Size: Average 2–20lb (1–9kg), up to over 100lb (45kg).

There is no mistaking the adult barracuda with its large line-cutting teeth and the black blotches on the silvery lower flanks. However there are three very small relatives which look like juvenile great barracuda, but lack the blotches. These include the almost identical northern sennet (*Sphyraena borealis*), which is often caught in mid-Atlantic and Gulf estuaries when the waters are warm, and the southern sennet (*Sphyraena picudilla*). These fish only grow to about

15in (38cm), while the guaguanche (*Sphyraena guachancho*) features a yellow or golden stripe and grows to 2ft (60cm).

These small members of the family readily strike lures and baits almost as big as they are, and are safe to eat. However, the great barracuda is one of the fish most likely to carry ciguatera poisoning in areas where it is common. That's a shame because, despite the smelly slime on their skins, barracuda have fine white meat and are consumed almost everywhere outside the US – even where the natives understand that they're literally playing Russian roulette with their meal. The cautious angler should avoid eating cuda larger than a few pounds in weight, particularly if they're caught from the reefs.

BELOW: Barracuda in shallow waters love to strike tube lures reeled rapidly across the surface.

THE SNAPPER FAMILY
Lutjanidae

This family of warm-water bottom fish includes some of the world's finest eating fish. Many of the snappers are far from sedentary bottom species, often rising to chase live baits on the surface over reefs and even feeding on the flats. More than 250 species are found throughout the world, but only a few are important in North American waters. Characteristics of the family include large mouths with eyes set high on the head; pointed pectoral fins; 10 spines in the first dorsal, which is joined to the second dorsal; two or three spines in the anal fin; and a distinct lateral line and large scales.

The most common snapper is the gray, or mangrove (*Lutjanus griseus*), which frequents shallow waters and can be spotted swimming around the south Florida docks. Though not colorful, this wary fish shows a broad dark stripe from the snout tip through the eye when excited.

The yellowtail snapper (*Ocyurus chrysurus*) is aptly named and can't be confused with any other. It is the most common snapper of the Keys reefs, but has been overfished in Bermuda and most Caribbean Islands.

DATA

Habitat: Offshore waters.

Habits: Bottom feeder.

Range: Atlantic from North Carolina to Brazil, plus the Caribbean and Gulf of Mexico.

Size: Average 5–15lb (2–7kg), up to 50lb (20kg).

Red Snapper

Lutjanus campechanus

This bright red fish is the most important of all the snappers from a commercial viewpoint. It isn't great sport in the 40 fathom or greater depths it frequents, but the species supports a large party-boat fishery from Gulf of Mexico ports. Some are also caught by party boats fishing along the Atlantic coast from North Carolina to Florida, but in many cases other species are falsely identified as reds. The true red snapper is a very distinct stocky fish with not only red sides but also red fins and eyes. The commercial pressure on this species in the Gulf has severely reduced the population and led to various restrictions.

Mutton Snapper

Lutjanus analis

The mutton is a reef and inshore species which is often found on the flats. Though somewhat reddish (and often mis-labeled as red snapper), it has other colors on it – including an olive-green back; small blue streaks on the head, back, and flanks; reddish to orangeish fins; and a black, oval-shaped spot on the upper flank of each side.

DATA

Habitat: Inshore waters/reefs/flats.

Habits: Bottom to mid feeder.

Range: Both coasts of Florida, the Bahamas, and south through the Caribbean to Brazil.

Size: Average 3–12lb (1–5kg), up to 30lb (13kg).

Mutton snappers are fine game and food fish which will strike jigs, live and dead baits and even flies.

THE SEA BASS FAMILY
Serranidae

This large family includes many small bottom-dwelling fish of little interest to anglers, but also the very important groupers and the black sea bass (which will be covered later). Even smaller versions of the black sea bass are common in the Gulf of Mexico and from North Carolina to northern Florida, but both the bank sea bass (*Centropristis ocyurus*) and rock sea bass (*Centropristis philadelphica*) rarely exceed a foot (around 30cm) in length.

Most serranids (including all the groupers and sea bass) are hermaphrodites. They begin life as females and change to males as they grow larger. Groupers tend to be territorial, living around obstructions on the bottom which constitute an area of

refuge to which they'll immediately retreat when hooked. Catching the larger specimens requires stout tackle and an intense effort to prevent the line from being cut off. Many groupers are tough fighters, and some will chase lures right to the surface.

The groupers have caudal fins which are rounded or squared off, a lower jaw which protrudes, and usually 11 dorsal spines. Grouper identifications are difficult, as all are capable of color change, making that an unreliable guide from area to area.

These bottom-dwelling fish are all good to eat, though a few of the larger types (particularly the yellowfin grouper) have been associated with ciguatera poisoning where that is common.

LEFT: The author with a jewfish, one of the largest of the bottom dwelling grouper family.

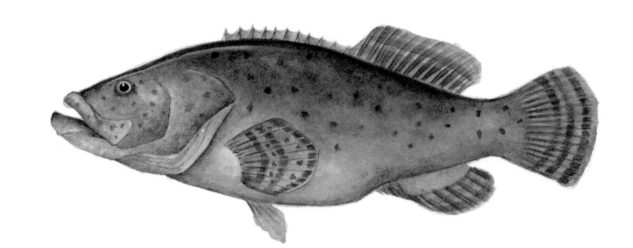

This is the largest of the groupers, and also the most pressured of the genus. These fearless shallow-water fish are such easy targets for divers that the fishery has been completely closed down in order to permit the long-lived fish to recover. Jewfish are most abundant around wrecks in the Gulf of Mexico off south-west Florida, but also tend to lay under bridges and docks, in channels and even in holes on the Florida Keys flats. Small jewfish are common in the mangrove areas and rivers of Florida's west coast. The brown body of this large-mouthed

Jewfish

Epinephelus itajara

grouper is covered with spots and blotches – and it has 4–5 irregular, broad, diagonal dark brown bands. Jewfish are hooked on both live and dead baits, and must be muscled away from wherever they live or the angler will be cut off in short order. Smaller jewfish are more active and will even strike at jigs.

DATA

Habitat: Inshore waters/bays/flats/rivers/wrecks.

Habits: Bottom feeder.

Range: Florida to Brazil, plus the Gulf of Mexico and Caribbean.

Size: Average 10–100lb (4.5–45kg), up to 800lb (363kg).

Nassau Grouper

Epinephelus striatus

DATA

Habitat: Reefs.

Habits: Bottom feeder.

Range: North Carolina to Brazil, plus Gulf of Mexico and Bermuda.

Size: Average 3–10lb (1.3–4.5kg), up to 55lb (25kg).

A common shallow-water species, the Nassau is most abundant in the Bahamas. It's a handsome grouper which is easily identified by the large black saddle-like blotch always present between the soft dorsal and caudal fins. It exhibits many color variations but has dark bars on the head and body, and black dots around the eyes. Nassaus are fine game fish which frequent coral heads and reef areas and respond readily to live baits and lures.

It is highly esteemed as a food fish.

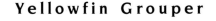

Yellowfin Grouper

Mycteroperca venehosa

Though the color of this grouper is highly variable, the outer third of the pectoral fin is a bright yellow or orange. It also has dark brown blotches arranged in lengthwise rows, extending into the caudal fin, and numerous small, dark reddish spots. The yellowfin is particularly abundant on the reefs of the Bahamas, and will respond to jigs and trolled lures as well as baits.

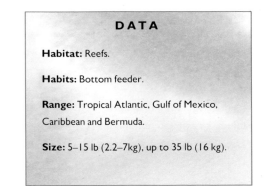

Red Hind

Epinephelus guttatus

DATA

Habitat: Reefs.

Habits: Bottom feeder.

Range: Florida to Brazil, plus southern Gulf of Mexico, Caribbean, and Bermuda.

Size: Average ½–2lb (0.2–1kg), up to 4lb (2kg).

Unending numbers of red hind can be jigged on reefs in the Bahamas. The reddish body is covered with large red spots, and the outer portions of the soft dorsal, caudal, and anal fins are blackish – sometimes with very narrow, pale edges. The similar rock hind (*Epinephelus adscensionis*) has more coloration over orange-brown spots and a saddle-like black blotch between the dorsal and caudal fins. Rock hind are common on the Gulf of Mexico snapper banks and shallow rocky bottoms in the Bahamas.

DATA

Habitat: Reefs.

Habits: Bottom feeder.

Range: Tropical Atlantic, Gulf of Mexico, Caribbean and Bermuda.

Size: 5–15 lb (2.2–7kg), up to 35 lb (16 kg).

THE PORGY FAMILY
Sparidae

Members of this large family are found over much of the world, primarily in warmer waters. Typically, they have compressed bodies with eyes located high on the head. The second (soft) dorsal and anal fins are relatively large and about the same shape. All of the North American porgies are relatively small fish but the family includes much larger species common in South Africa, such as the red steenbras, which may grow

to 200lb (91kg). The most important family member (in terms of commercial and recreational landings) is the scup, a northern fish to be covered under "Atlantic Coolwater Species."

LEFT: A good-sized sheepshead from Marco, Florida.

Sheepshead

Archosargus probatocephalus

The largest of the North American porgies is impossible to confuse with any other species. It sports alternating broad bands of black and silver on its compressed sides, and a small mouth armed with protruding, flat teeth which are used to crush the shells of mollusks and crustaceans. The IGFA world record (to 1990) is a 21¼-pounder (9.6kg) taken at Bayou St John, New Orleans, Louisiana on April 16, 1982 by Wayne Desselle. During the previous century this species was abundant enough in New York

that the famed party-boat port of Sheepshead Bay was named for it. Yet, sheepshead are rarely caught there anymore, and are unusual north of Cape Hatteras. However, they remain a common inshore species further south along the Atlantic coast and all through the Gulf of Mexico.

Sheepshead are found around piers, jetties, and other obstructions, as well as on oyster bars – and can be taken with a variety of baits, though fiddler crabs and shrimp are the usual choices. They bite lightly and are difficult to hook, making them a real challenge for the angler. Sheepshead are also powerful fighters and fine food fish.

DATA

Habitat: Bays/rivers.

Habits: Bottom feeder.

Range: North Carolina to Brazil, plus the Gulf of Mexico and West Indies.

Size: Average 2–5lb (1–2.2kg), up to over 30lb (13.5kg).

IGFA Record: 21¼lb (9.6kg), Louisiana, USA, 1982.

Jolthead Porgy

Calamus bajonado

DATA

Habitat: Inshore to offshore waters.

Habits: Bottom feeder.

Range: North Carolina to Brazil, plus Bermuda, Gulf of Mexico, and West Indies.

Size: Average 1–6lb (0.45–2.7kg), up to 25lb (11kg).

IGFA Record: 23¼lb (10.5kg) Florida, USA, 1990.

Though most biologists have postulated maximum sizes of only about 10lb (4.5kg) for this warm-water porgy, the IGFA has recognized a 23¼-pounder (10.5kg) caught in the Gulf of Mexico off Madeira Beach, Florida by Hakm M Wilder on March 14, 1990 as the world record.

Basically silvery in color, the jolthead also has brown blotches on the body which tend to disappear when it dies. A blue line runs below the eyes. The very similar red porgy (*Pagrus pagrus*) is an important deep-water species which fills the bags of customers on party boats sailing out of southern North Carolina ports. It can grow to about 12lb (5kg), and is often misnamed "silver snapper." In addition to its reddish-silver coloration with minute blue spots, the red porgy is distinguished by a rounded posterior nostril – whereas all other American porgies have slit-like posterior nostrils. The whitebone porgy (*Calamus leucosteus*) is the only other fairly large southern porgy. It's caught from North Carolina south and throughout the Gulf, and can grow to 18in (46cm). Whitebones have a silvery body with faint crossbars, and blue lines both over and under the eyes. In addition there are also dark blotches on the dorsal and anal fins.

The hogfish is the only important tropical member of the wrasse family (Labridae) which consists primarily of colorful, small reef fish plus the tautog and cunner of the north and the California sheepshead. Also frequently referred to by the misnomer of hog snapper, the hogfish is a distinctive red-orange fish with a pointed, steep snout, thick lips, and protruding canine teeth. The first 3–4 dorsal spines are extended into filaments, and the tips of the dorsal, anal, and caudal fins are pointed. A black spot is present on the aft portion of the dorsal fin where it meets the body. Hogfish are solitary fish which feed on mollusks, crustaceans and sea urchins. They're tough fighters and a great prize for reef anglers.

Hogfish are considered to be among the very best eating fish, but unfortunately they can also be involved in ciguatera poisoning where that toxin is a problem.

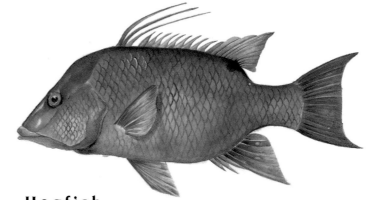

Hogfish

Lachnolaimus maximus

DATA

Habitat: Reefs.

Habits: Bottom feeder.

Range: North Carolina to Brazil, plus Bermuda and the Caribbean.

Size: Average 3–6lb (1.3–2.7kg), up to 45lb (20kg).

Somewhat similar is the Spanish hogfish (*Bodianus rufus*), which looks about the same except for the lack of filaments – but is even more striking in appearance. The forward portion of the fish is crimson, while the rear is bright yellow. Found primarily on shallow coral reefs in the tropics from Florida south, and also Bermuda and offshore reefs in the northern Gulf of Mexico, this species grows only to about 3lb (1.3kg) but is an excellent food fish.

Queen Triggerfish

Balistes vetula

Triggerfish and tilefish make up the leatherjacket family, Balistidae. They are characterized by tough skins, and the triggers are so-named because the long first spine of the dorsal fin is locked into place by the shorter second spine – but can be lowered by depressing the even shorter third spine, or "trigger." The leathery skin has no slime on it, and the soft dorsal and anal fins are of about the same size and shape. The queen triggerfish has filaments which extend from the soft dorsal and caudal fins, but this fish cannot be confused with any other by its coloring alone. It appears to be a creation of Picasso's with the orange and blue colors, and two broad, curved blue bands on the head. Queen triggerfish aren't too common in Florida, but are very abundant on reefs in the Bahamas. They will readily hit small baits and jigs. Queen triggers are strong fighters on light tackle. They make fine eating after the skin is removed.

DATA

Habitat: Reefs.

Habits: Bottom to mid feeder.

Range: Florida to Brazil, plus Bermuda and the Caribbean.

Size: Average 1–3lb (0.45–1.3kg), up to 12lb (5.4kg).

IGFA Record: 12lb (5.4kg) Florida, USA, 1985.

Also of angling interest are the gray triggerfish (*Balistes capriscus*) and the ocean triggerfish (*Canthidermis sufflamen*). The gray is a wide-ranging species which is common around Gulf of Mexico oil rigs and reefs, and can be found as far north as Cape Cod during the summer – where it's frequently caught by near-shore bottom anglers off New York and New Jersey in August and September. The ocean triggerfish has prolonged outer caudal rays, and is usually encountered in offshore waters. They're often spotted around floating objects, and will nip at live balao being slow-trolled for sailfish in the Gulf Stream off south-east Florida. Ocean triggers in the 5lb (2.2kg) class are common, and biologists feel they may be the largest species in the family.

Gafftopsail Catfish

Bagre marinus

The sea catfish family Ariidae includes two Atlantic species with typical catfish bodies, featuring slimy skin without scales, and sharp serrated spines on the dorsal and pectoral fins which can inflict painful wounds. They also incubate orally, with the males carrying the fertilized eggs in their mouths. The gafftopsail features elongated first rays of the dorsal and pectoral fins. It has two barbels on the lower jaw, and a blueish coloration on the back. The dried skull is in the shape of a cross, which appears to carry a figure on it. Gafftopsails

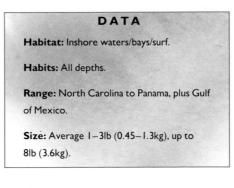

DATA

Habitat: Inshore waters/bays/surf.

Habits: All depths.

Range: North Carolina to Panama, plus Gulf of Mexico.

Size: Average 1–3lb (0.45–1.3kg), up to 8lb (3.6kg).

are good game and food fish, which are very common in the bays and surf of Florida and the Gulf states. They'll readily hit plugs and jigs as well as baits.

Similar in shape but quite different in many ways is the hardhead catfish (*Arius felis*), also commonly called sea catfish. This dull greenish species has four barbels and no elongated fins. It's one of the most common inshore species in the South Atlantic and Gulf, but is regarded as a pest. While edible, they are not regarded very highly as a food fish.

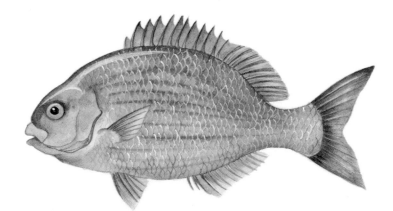

Bermuda Chub

Kyphosus sectatrix

DATA

Habitat: Inshore waters/reefs.

Habits: All depths.

Range: Florida to Brazil, plus Bermuda and the Caribbean.

Size: Average 1–3lb (0.45–1.3kg), up to 20lb (9kg).

The only important Atlantic member of the sea chub family Kyphosidae, the Bermuda chub is a schooling fish with an ovate, somewhat compressed body. Though basically gray, it has two yellow bands on the head and lengthwise brassy bands along the body. Owing to their tiny mouths, small baits and hooks must be used to tempt this fine game and food fish.

Tripletail

Lobotes surinamensis

DATA

Habitat: Inshore waters.

Habits: Surface feeder.

Range: North Carolina to Argentina, plus the Caribbean and Gulf of Mexico.

Size: Average 2–5lb (1–2.2kb), up to 50lb (22kg).

The only western Atlantic member of the small tripletail family Lobotidae is so-called because the rounded second dorsal and anal fins extend backward along the caudal peduncle making it appear that the fish has three tails. This is a lazy brownish fish with a sloping forehead. It usually hangs around obstructions, which can be as small as the bouys for lobster and crab pots. It frequently floats on its sides, appearing to be a dead leaf. Tripletails are good food fish, and strong fighters which will readily attack jigs and live baits. Many anglers specialize in this fishing along the Gulf coast of Florida.

Atlantic Coolwater Inshore Species

The species covered in this section are those which are caught primarily in inshore waters to the north of Cape Hatteras. Many of these fish (such as the weakfish, summer flounder, and black sea bass) are quite common south of that point, but all are most abundant and of greatest importance to the north. Other species which are common up to Chesapeake Bay (such as the red drum, cobia, amberjack, king mackerel, and spot) and even up to Delaware Bay (such as the black drum) are included under "Atlantic and Gulf of Mexico Warmwater Inshore Species" since they are basically warmwater fish. Many other species described in that section are frequently encountered during late summer as far north as Cape Cod, when water temperatures are at their highest. Since federal restrictions were placed on netting of Spanish mackerel, that species has rebounded and become increasingly common at the northern end of its range, particularly off the northern New Jersey coast. Gray triggerfish are regularly caught by bottom fishers off the New Jersey and New York coasts every summer, and the young of most southern species are commonly found around mid-Atlantic docks during late summer.

Striped Bass

Morone saxatilis

This most important inshore game and food fish of the temperate bass family Perci-chthyidae has been introduced throughout much of the United States. An anadromous species which is as much at home in fresh water as in salt, the striper is now caught by anglers in such landlocked states as Nebraska, Oklahoma, Pennsylvania, Arkansas, Tennessee and Arizona just as it is along the Atlantic and Pacific coasts. The "classic" striped bass is the migratory population which ranges from the Outer Banks of North Carolina to Nova Scotia. Chesapeake Bay is the prime spawning area for the species which is called rock, or rockfish, in that area. Spawning also occurs in the Hudson and Delaware Rivers, but successful reproduction has not been documented during recent years in New England rivers – though the Nova Scotia and New Brunswick populations are thought to be self-sustaining.

Identification is not a problem with striped bass: 7 to 8 prominent black stripes run along the silvery sides, while the belly is white and the back can be various colors – ranging from green in river fish to steel-blue or black. Migratory bass often have a light purple sheen on the back which is more prominent in the larger fish. The dorsal fins are separated giving a good identifica-tion factor in juveniles, which are similar to the closely related white perch. Hybridiza-tion of the striper has been extensive, and the whiterock or sunshine bass cross with the freshwater white bass has been widely stocked into lakes. It is a stockier fish with broken stripes.

Stripers are the most esteemed coastal species from Virginia to Maine, and angling pressure is intense on a fish which can be caught in many fashions and with any tackle under a wide variety of conditions. School stripers provide fine sport in areas as accessible as the piers in New York Harbor, and they can prosper even in waters as polluted as the East River. Trophy bass of 50lb (22kg) or more are caught primarily from surf, bay and near-shore ocean waters.

DATA

Habitat: Inshore waters/bays/surf/rivers.

Habits: All depths.

Range: Nova Scotia and New Brunswick to northern Florida, plus California, Oregon, and many lakes and rivers.

Size: Average 4–15lb (1.8–6.8kg), up to 125lb (57kg).

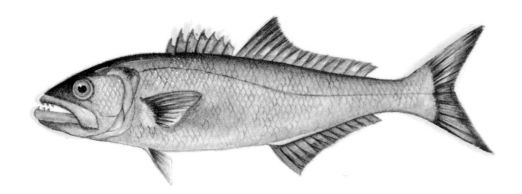

Bluefish

Pomatomus salatrix

> **DATA**
>
> **Habitat:** Inshore to offshore waters/bays/ rivers/surf.
>
> **Habits:** All depths.
>
> **Range:** Worldwide in temperate and some tropical waters, but not in the eastern Pacific.
>
> **Size:** Average 1–10lb (0.45–4.5kg), up to 35lb (15.8kg).
>
> **IGFA Record:** 31¾lb (15.7kg) North Carolina, USA, 1972.

While the striped bass may be the most esteemed inshore game fish of the north-east US, the bluefish is the most popular in terms of angler participation and catch. The numbers taken by sportfishers usually exceed those of any other species, and the total weight (estimated at 69.6 thousand metric tons along the Atlantic Coast in 1980) has been far greater than that of any other saltwater recreational fishery in the US for many years. Though distributed widely over the world, this sole member of the family Pomatomidae is probably nowhere as abundant as in the north-eastern US. Bluefish are also important from Cape Hatteras to Florida, and are caught in lesser quantities throughout the Gulf of Mexico.

The Atlantic migratory population includes bluefish which sweep up the coast from southern Florida to North Carolina in the spring, and others which move from North Carolina or offshore waters into mid-Atlantic and New England waters from May to November before returning to their wintering areas. Spawning takes place offshore, and the young grow up in bays and rivers where they attain sizes of 6–10in (15–25cm) by late summer and early fall. The young-of-the-year are called snappers, and provide a panfishery for youngsters using light tackle and small baits or lures.

The bluefish is a rather bland-looking fish with a greenish blue back blending to a silvery blue on the upper sides, to a white belly. The most prominent feature is the moderately pointed snout with an under-slung, slightly protruding jaw armed with small but razor-sharp teeth which can cut fingers to the bone as easily as they chop off lines and cut bait fish in half. The nickname "choppers" is well-deserved in the bluefish's case, and sea birds are attracted to easy pickings in their feeding areas.

Most bluefish live for 10 to 15 years and can attain weights of 20lb (9kg) or more. They are very cyclical, and over the years have virtually disappeared from vast areas of the coast for decades. They were scarce when I was a child, but started building up again in the late 1950s and have been abundant ever since. Their size increased steadily every year in the 1960s and reached a peak on January 30, 1972 when James M Hussey trolled a 31¾-pounder (15.7kg) in Hatteras Inlet, NC. Blues in the 20–25lb (9–11kg) class are still caught every year, but no one has come close to that IGFA record since then. There have long been rumors of much larger bluefish (up to 45lb (20kg) being available in the Mediterranean and off north-west Africa and the Azores, but every IGFA line-class record as of 1990 still comes from the area from North Carolina to Massachusetts, except for the former world record 24lb 3oz (10.9kg) blue caught in the Azores in 1953.

The bluefish may well be the ideal game fish in that it responds readily to a wide range of bait and lures, fights hard, jumps, is good eating, and is very abundant. Anglers in the north-east have become spoiled over the last few decades by a species which is almost too easy to catch – and many sport-fishers have grown to hate them because they tear up lures and baits fished for striped bass, weakfish, sharks, and tuna. However, this fishery is the envy of small game anglers over the rest of the world, and its disappearance would create havoc in the mid-Atlantic – especially in New York Bight, which produces about 50 per cent of the catch and where party boats fish for them day and night during a long season.

Bluefish are caught by just about any method imaginable. Chumming with ground mossbunker is very popular in New York Bight, and vast numbers are also caught from party, charter, and private boats by dropping diamond jigs over schools and retrieving at a high rate of speed. Trolling is also very effective, and some of the largest blues are caught on live mossbunkers or other live baits.

The Mid-Atlantic Fishery Management Council Bluefish Plan that became effective in 1990 placed a 10-fish limit on anglers fishing in federal waters (beyond 3 miles/ 4.8km offshore) and limited the commercial catch to no more than 20 per cent of the recreational harvest. Some States have implemented a similar 10-bluefish limit.

Bluefish flesh is oily, but quite tasty. However, it deteriorates rapidly and doesn't freeze well – factors which have prevented massive commercial exploitation. In some areas there's a late season problem with excessive PCB accumulation in large bluefish. However, any concern can be eliminated by skinning the fish, cutting away the belly flaps and dark meat, and broiling or baking so the fat drips away.

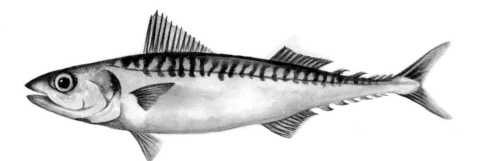

Atlantic Mackerel

Scomber scombrus

> **DATA**
>
> **Habitat:** Inshore to offshore waters.
>
> **Habits:** All depths (primarily mid and surface feeder).
>
> **Range:** Cape Hatteras to Labrador.
>
> **Size:** Average ½lb to 2lb (200g to 1kg), up to 7½lb (3.4kg).

This most common mackerel of the North Atlantic is one of the most abundant species in the world. Atlantic mackerel have always been somewhat cyclical in abundance. However, those swings weren't a problem until Soviet and other foreign trawlers targeted the species for several years during the 1960s and early 1970s. It took many years of conservation under a Mid-Atlantic Fishery Management Council plan before mackerel populations returned to levels approaching those of the past. But by 1990 the schools were so large that the National Marine Fisheries Service was once again considering them an under-utilized species.

Mackerel winter in offshore waters, but start moving inshore even before spring. If the waters are warm enough, schools may be found outside Chesapeake Bay by late-February – though March is more normal. They then start a spawning run up the coast, usually arriving off Delaware Bay by the beginning of April. The Metropolitan New York–New Jersey area normally gets a two-to-three-week shot at the mackerel from about mid-April to early-May, and then the schools rapidly move to the east.

Another group of mackerel winter further north and move inshore in the spring to populate all northern areas. Though mackerel almost invariably remain at least a few miles offshore to the south, they are commonly encountered right up into bays and harbors in New England. Another run occurs in the fall as the schools move to the south, but relatively little sportfishing is done for them at that time except by party boats during December and January in the Metropolitan New York–New Jersey area.

Very small Atlantic mackerel are called tinkers, and they're frequently caught in interior waters. However, they're also confused with another small member of the family – the chub mackerel (*Scomber japonicus*), which is also found in the Pacific. The chub is usually less than a foot in length, though it grows to over 2lb (1kg), and is most common in offshore waters where they often rise to the surface in great numbers under lights at night. The Atlantic mackerel has 20 to 23 blackish, nearly vertical, wavy bars on the back and no spots below these bars. On the other hand, the chub has about 30 bars which break into a series of dusky spots at about the lateral line. Internally, the chub has an air bladder while the Atlantic mackerel does not.

Atlantic mackerel are excellent fighting fish, but are usually caught several at a time on tackle which is much too heavy for their size. When a boat is positioned over a school, bags can be filled quickly with these fish by dropping down rigs with several tiny tubes or feathers and a diamond jig or lead weight. Though good-eating as a fresh fish, they are no longer as favored in the US as overseas. However, mackerel are highly-esteemed by larger predators and make excellent live and cut baits for sharks, tuna, striped bass, bluefish, etc.

THE COD FAMILY
Gadidae

This family of coldwater fishes is of great commercial value in both the North Atlantic and North Pacific, but only of sporting interest in the former. Cod, pollock, and haddock are the basic offshore bottom fish for New England anglers, and the first two are also seasonally very important in New Jersey and New York. All members of the family have elongated bodies and spineless fins with the ventral fins being located far forward, usually ahead of the pectorals.

LEFT: Michael Ristori with one of the most important foodfish of the Atlantic, the cod.

Atlantic Cod

Gadus morhua

This giant of the family is one of the most important and familiar fish of American and Canadian waters. Their great value in colonial times is attested to by their inclusion in the colonial seal of Massachusetts and the gilded carving of the "Sacred Cod" which hangs in the State House in Boston. The cod was also placed on a bank note in Nova Scotia with the inscription "Success to the Fisheries".

Cod have three dorsal and two anal fins plus a square, slightly concave tail. Body color is usually brownish or greenish with numerous dark spots, but cod living over kelp assume a rusty color. A light lateral line rises along the body above the first anal fin, and the head is cone shaped with a large barbel on the chin. The cod's mouth is large and contains many small teeth which will rough up a monofilament leader, but won't cut it.

The largest cod ever recorded was a 211½lb (96kg) specimen over six feet (1.8m) long which was taken in a trawl off northern Massachusetts in May, 1895. There are also records of other cod from 100lb (45kg) to 175lb (79kg) being caught prior to the turn of the century, but such sizes haven't been reported in recent years. The closest is the IGFA world record of 98¾lb (44.8kg), taken at Isle of Shoals, New Hampshire on June 8, 1969 by Alphonse J

DATA

Habitat: Inshore to offshore waters.

Habits: Bottom feeder.

Range: Both sides of North Atlantic, and Virginia to Greenland in the Western Atlantic.

Size: Average 3–30lb (1.3–13.6kg), up to 211½lb (96kg).

IGFA Record: 98¾lb (44.8kg), New Hampshire, USA, 1969.

Bielevich. A very few other cod of over 80lb (36kg) have been caught on rod and reel, including two in the mid-Atlantic – an 81-pounder (36.7kg) out of Brielle, NJ and an 85-pounder (38.5kg) at Montauk, NY. While cod up to 50lb (22kg) aren't that unusual, any larger than that can be considered a real trophy.

The drop in maximum size of the cod probably relates to the intense pressure placed on the species by commercial fishing. There was a huge decline in population levels during the 1970s after the foreign fishing fleets targeted cod and haddock for a few years, but some good year-classes after the US 200-mile (322km) fishing limit was instituted in 1977 brought the fishery back. However, the constant expansion of the American and Canadian trawler fleets, and a proliferation of bottom gill nets, has once again put a big dent in the population which the New England Fishery Management Council has been unable to stem with various management plans. Eventually this overfishing will have to be stopped, and the very prolific cod will probably return to reasonable abundance. A 75lb (34kg) cod was found to contain 9,100,000 eggs, and if all of those were able to hatch and mature we'd soon be walking across the ocean on their backs!

Cod favor rough bottoms, but can be found even over open bottoms when food is abundant. They'll eat almost anything at times, and can be quite fast and aggressive when rising in the water column to chase launce (sand eels), herring, and mackerel. Normally caught by bottom fishing with clams, squid, or cut bait, they also hit diamond jigs readily at times.

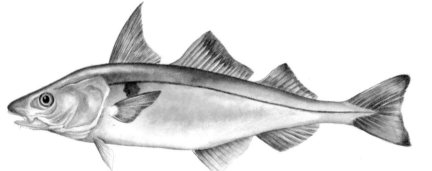

Pollock

Pollachius virens

Pollock are more aggressive and harder fighting fish than the cod, and they're usually found higher in the water column. A more solid-looking fish than the cod, it also has a slightly projecting lower jaw, forked tail and a light, fairly straight lateral line. The color is generally olive green to brownish green, and there are no conspicuous marks. The chin barbel is either tiny or completely missing in older fish.

Pollock feed on schooling fish such as squid, mackerel, and sand launce rather than grubbing along bottom. As a result, diamond jigs account for most of the sporting catch. However, pollock will take dead baits such as squid and even clams at times. The use of squid at night over the deepwater wrecks is especially effective.

Whereas pollock are almost exclusively caught on wrecks in New York Bight, they occupy a variety of habitats from Block Is-

land east and north. Into the 1960s there was even a small spring run in the Montauk surf, and quite a few were trolled in the rips off that point. But that fishing has faded

DATA

Habitat: Inshore to offshore waters.

Habits: Bottom feeder.

Range: Both sides of North Atlantic, and in western Atlantic from New Jersey to Greenland.

Size: Average 5–30lb (2.2–13.6kg), up to 70lb (31.7kg).

IGFA Record: 46lb 7oz (21kg), New Jersey, USA, 1975.

into history. However, large pollock can be caught on ledges off Block Island in the spring and at Nantucket Shoals as well as the deepwater wrecks such as the Andrea Doria off Nantucket. Greater numbers are boated north of Cape Cod, especially on offshore banks from northern Massachusetts to Maine. Juvenile pollock, known as harbor pollock, are caught in great numbers from northern New England docks and inshore grounds. These 1–3lb (0.45–1.3kg) fish are great sport on light tackle and readily hit small metal lures.

Though a fine food fish, pollock isn't rated as highly as cod or haddock, as the flesh is somewhat softer and doesn't keep as well. In New England they're often marketed as "Boston bluefish".

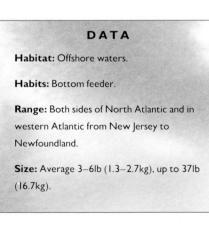

Very similar in shape to the pollock, this bottom fish is instantly identified by the almost straight black lateral line and the prominent black patch on the side between the lateral line and the pectoral fin. The back color is purplish gray, becoming silver-gray below, and white on the belly. Unlike the cod, it prefers open bottoms, rather than wrecks and rough terrain. Small baits, such as clams, squid and cut fish, presented on the bottom will do the job.

Haddock are the most northern of the cod family, rarely being taken in New York Bight any longer – though quite a few were

Haddock

Melanogrammus aeglefinus

DATA

Habitat: Offshore waters.

Habits: Bottom feeder.

Range: Both sides of North Atlantic and in western Atlantic from New Jersey to Newfoundland.

Size: Average 3–6lb (1.3–2.7kg), up to 37lb (16.7kg).

caught there several decades ago. They're also now a rare catch at Montauk, though a few are mixed in with cod catches at Little Georges Bank. Haddock are much more common from Nantucket Shoals and Chatham north and east, with quite a few being caught from party boats out of Gloucester, Massachusetts. The commercial catch comes primarily from Georges Bank and the Grand Banks.

Haddock are highly regarded as food fish, and were terribly depleted by the foreign fleets in the 1960s. Unfortunately, after making a comeback, the American and Canadian trawlers have continued the overfishing and left little surplus for anglers. This species has always been more cyclical than the other members of the family, and in years of scarcity is rarely seen in nearshore waters.

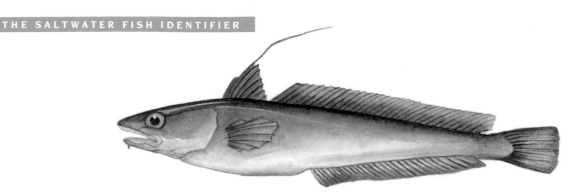

Red Hake

Urophycis chuss

> **DATA**
>
> **Habitat:** Inshore to offshore waters/surf.
>
> **Habits:** Bottom to mid feeder.
>
> **Range:** Virginia to Newfoundland.
>
> **Size:** Average 1–3lb (0.45–1.3kg), up to 8lb (3.6kg).

Formerly known as squirrel hake, this species is invariably called ling in New York Bight. Though caught commercially in great numbers from eastern Long Island to north of Cape Cod, it is of no recreational interest except practically at the end of its southerly range in the New York metropolitan area. Vast numbers are caught there by bottom anglers year-round.

Red hake, which are also common in the party-boat catch south to Cape May, NJ, have soft reddish to brownish bodies and are often yellowish on the underside. The third ray in the dorsal fin is elongate, and it has very long second dorsal and anal fins. The long ventral fins look like feelers and reach to the anal fin. These sluggish bottom feeders will eat almost any small bait.

They are a fine eating fish if cleaned promptly and iced down, but when improperly handled the soft flesh has led to such names as "sewer trout". A very similar inshore relative is the spotted hake (*Urophycis regia*) which is often caught in the New York Bight surf or by fluke fishermen. This species, which grows to only 1½lb (0.68kg), lacks the extended dorsal fin of the red hake and has an alternating black and white lateral line. The similar white hake (*Urophycis tenuis*) looks like an overgrown red hake, but sports a purplish sheen. It grows to at least 60lb (27kg), and is found on deepwater wrecks from New Jersey north, with great numbers occupying the 240 foot (78m) depths in which the Andrea Doria rests off Nantucket.

Silver Hake

Merluccius bilinearis

> **DATA**
>
> **Habitat:** Inshore to offshore waters/surf.
>
> **Habits:** Bottom feeder.
>
> **Range:** Virginia to Gulf of St Lawrence.
>
> **Size:** Average ½–2lb (0.2–1kg), up to 8lb (3.6kg).

This hake bears little resemblance to the rest of the cod family with its silvery sides, large mouth full of sharp teeth, and lack of any barbel. It's a common continental shelf species from New Jersey to New England, but is ignored as a recreational species except in the New York metropolitan area. Like the red hake, it makes spring and fall inshore migrations, but these aren't nearly as dependable – and they then may range far offshore in summer and midwinter rather than staying in the depths of the Mud Hole. Silver hake are called whiting in the mid-Atlantic, and are a very important target for the party-boat fleets of New York Bight from December to April.

The big run usually occurs in December and January, with silver hake flooding into inshore waters in vast schools. They bite both day and night, but are most active in shallower waters after dark. At that time they may also move right into the surf to chase small bait fish. During years of great abundance this pursuit may result in their being thrown up on the beach by waves. They freeze on the spot in the mid-winter cold and can be picked up – leading to the nickname "frostfish". These aggressive fish will hit diamond jigs and other lures, but are generally caught on strips of squid, mackerel, herring or another silver hake. Multiple hook rigs are fished in order to catch as many of the small fish on each drop as possible.

Silver hake are a firm fish with tasty white meat, and are excellent for smoking. In 1989 they were the number one commercial finfish catch in the mid-Atlantic area by weight (16.7 million lb/7.58 million kg) though their value per pound is low.

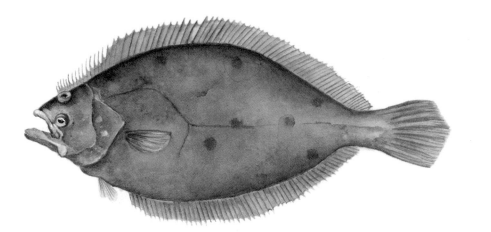

Summer Flounder

Paralichthys dentatus

This most important inshore bottom fish of the mid-Atlantic often challenges for the lead in numbers caught by anglers in that region. However, it's also a valuable food fish which is under enormous year-round pressure by commercial fishing (primarily trawlers) in addition to the seasonal effort by anglers when the flatfish are inshore. Bad spawning years in the prime Virginia waters from 1987-9 reduced summer flounder populations to very low levels, which has led to management plans restricting both commercial and sportfishing activities in the future. A 14in (35.5cm) minimum

---

DATA

Habitat: Inshore waters/bays/rivers.

Habits: Bottom feeder.

Range: Cape Cod to South Carolina.

Size: Average 1–4lb (0.2–1.8kg), up to 25lb (11.3kg).

---

size has been in effect from New York north, and a new management plan will extend that limit south to North Carolina.

The summer flounder is the only important north-eastern member of the lefteye flounder family Bothidae. It is referred to simply as flounder from Delaware Bay south, but is known as fluke to the north – where "flounder" means the winter flounder.

Summer flounders move inshore during the spring and spread along the coast and into bays and rivers. They start going back offshore in September and spawn in the fall. These fish have large mouths armed with teeth, and are quite aggressive when chasing small fish in the shallows. Fluke will even occasionally take lures. This brown flounder can't be confused with any other in the mid-Atlantic, but south of Hatteras it mixes with the southern flounder, from which it can be distinguished by the regularly placed small spot on the eyed side.

Fluke are usually sold in the filleted form, and that white meat is regularly mislabeled as fillet of sole.

Winter Flounder

Pseudopleuronectes americanus

This is the most important of the north-eastern members of the righteyed flounder family Pleuronectidae. Though a small fish, it is quite meaty and makes excellent eating. Winter flounders fill in nicely around the summer flounder in the mid-Atlantic. As the fluke head offshore in the fall, winter flounder move into bays and rivers before over-wintering in soft bottoms. As the first warming occurs, they start becoming active again. Spawning is accomplished before they head back offshore for the summer.

Winter flounders have a tiny mouth and vary in color greatly, though they are usually brown or rusty with small dark spots. The similar yellowtail flounder (*Limanda ferruginea*) is strictly an offshore flounder rarely caught on hook and line. It has large irregular rusty spots on the eyed side and a lateral line

DATA

Habitat: Bays/rivers.

Habits: Bottom feeder.

Range: Delaware to Gulf of St Lawrence.

Size: Average ½–1lb (0.2–0.45kg), up to 10lb (4.5kg).

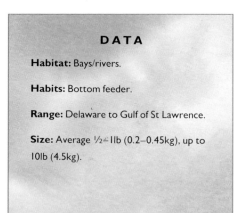

which arches over the pectoral fin, compared to the straight lateral line of the winter flounder. The caudal and edges of the dorsal and anal fins of the yellowtail are yellow. Large winter flounders tend to develop yellow coloration on the edges of the white side, and anglers think they've caught a yellowtail. Actually, the yellowtail is a very small species which rarely reaches 2lb (0.9kg) – and the lemon-hued winter flounders are sold at a premium as "lemon sole"

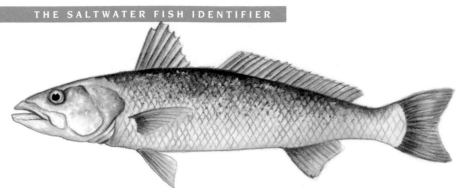

Whereas most of the drum family Sciaenidae prefers warmer waters, the weakfish is most abundant in the mid-Atlantic. Spring spawning runs of this trout look-alike occur in Chesapeake Bay, Delaware Bay, Great South and Peconic Bays, NY, and Narragansett Bay, RI. However, the species is cyclical, and very few weakfish have been appearing in Great South and Narragansett Bays during the late 1980s. Spawning runs in the other bays have also been greatly diminished, and there is fear that massive overfishing may once again reduce the population to the point it hit in the 1960s – when a weakfish of any size was an unusual catch north of Cape Hatteras.

From that low point, the population suddenly began rebounding in 1970. Within

Weakfish

Cynoscion regalis

DATA

Habitat: Inshore waters/bays/surf.

Habits: All depths.

Range: Cape Cod to Florida, and Gulf of Mexico.

Size: Average 2–10lb (0.9–4.5kg), up to 20lb (9kg).

a few years vast numbers of weakfish were being caught once again, and sizes increased until coolers were regularly being filled with 10–12lb (4.5–5.4kg) weaks in the spawning areas. The waste of this fine-

eating fish was as bad as before.

Weakfish populations below Cape Hatteras appear to be separate from the northern migratory groups, which winter at sea but enter the bays for spawning in April and May before spending the summer and fall in shallow near-shore, and surf or bay waters. Weakfish off southern North Carolina are abundant in shallow near-shore waters but don't enter the rivers and estuaries as do the spotted sea trout, and also tend to remain small.

The spotted sea trout becomes the dominant fish further south along the coast, and weakfish aren't abundant in the Gulf of Mexico. The two species are similarly shaped, but are easy to distinguish since the weak is peppered with small, almost indistinct spots primarily on the back but not on the fins, while the spotted sea trout has large black spots on its back, sides, and dorsal and caudal fins.

It's important to keep weakfish cold, and cook them promptly as the meat doesn't stand up well to freezing.

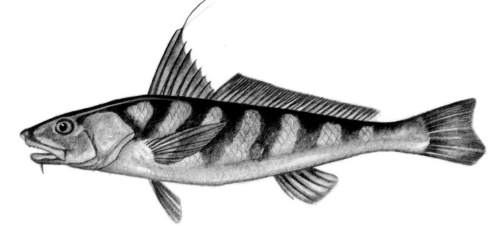

This beautiful little fish doesn't resemble most other members of the drum family Sciaenidae, and has no swim bladder with which to make noises. Like the southern and gulf kingfishes, it has a short barbel on the chin, a rounded snout with a tiny inferior mouth, and a long second dorsal fin which is more extended than those of its cousins. There are 7–8 dusky bands on the sides which are darker than those of the southern kingfish, and a diagonal bar on the nape forms a V-shaped mark with the first bar on

Northern Kingfish

Menticirrhus saxatilis

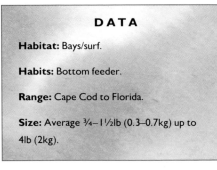

DATA

Habitat: Bays/surf.

Habits: Bottom feeder.

Range: Cape Cod to Florida.

Size: Average ¾–1½lb (0.3–0.7kg) up to 4lb (2kg).

the body, which doesn't occur in the southern kingfish. The northern kingfish ranges all the way into the Gulf of Mexico, but is most abundant from Chesapeake Bay north to New York; however it is largely replaced by the southern kingfish in the Carolinas.

A multitude of local names makes identification of this species difficult if you're just given a name. Northerners refer to it simply as kingfish (which can still confuse it with the king mackerel, which is called kingfish in the south), while it becomes roundhead, sea mink, and sea mullet further down the coast, and whiting in Florida (which confuses it with the silver hake, which is called whiting in the north). Indeed, scientists used to accept northern whiting or king whiting as the common name before the American Fisheries Society settled on northern kingfish.

Kingfish are among the best eating fish available in northern waters.

Atlantic Bonito

Sarda sarda

The bonito tribe Sardini is closely related to the tunas, but the fine-eating flesh is light colored and softer than that of their relatives. The Atlantic bonito is found throughout much of that ocean plus the Mediterranean and Black Seas, but is rare in the Caribbean and Gulf of Mexico. The IGFA all-tackle world record as of 1990 was an 18¼-pounder (8.2kg) caught in the Azores in 1953. Line-class records came from Madeira, the Canary Islands and Senegal, plus US areas ranging from Barnegat, New Jersey to Martha's Vineyard, Massachusetts. Larger bonito seem to be more common in the eastern Atlantic, and any over 10lb (4.5kg) are uncommon in the western Atlantic. Along the US Atlantic coast, bonito are mainly caught from New Jersey to Massachusetts. They are a summer fish, with large schools usually showing up in areas close to shore in July. Bonito can tolerate

---

DATA

Habitat: Inshore to offshore waters.

Habits: Mid to surface feeder.

Range: Atlantic Ocean, primarily from New Jersey to southern New England in the US.

Size: Average 3–7lb (1.3–3kg), up to about 20lb (9kg).

---

relatively cool waters, and may be caught in northern areas into early November.

Identification is very easy, since bonito have stripes on the back and not on the belly. They're also slimmer than the tunas, and have a mouth full of small, sharp teeth. Surprisingly, those teeth do less damage to mono than the less prominent teeth of the

tunas – and leaders are not required for this often line-shy species.

Bonito are fine game fish which are particularly important along the northern New Jersey coast from August into October, when they are taken from boats anchored on high spots located within a few miles of shore. A very light slick of mossbunker chum plus pieces of small bait fish, such as spearing, smelt, and sand lance, are used to attract the bonito, which are then caught on the bait fish placed on small, short-shanked hooks tied to light mono, or on very small jigs worked with a fast, whipping action. These fish provide great sport on light spinning and bait-casting gear, offering a miniaturized version of a fight with a large tuna on much heavier tackle.

Black Sea Bass

Centropristis striata

This is the only coolwater member of the large sea bass family Serranidae, which includes the groupers of the south Atlantic and Gulf of Mexico coasts. These handsome fish are among the most important bottom species of the mid-Atlantic for both sport and commercial anglers. They favor wrecks and rough bottoms while inshore, at which time they're vulnerable primarily only to hook-and-line and lobster or fish pots. However, sea bass are dragged up in large quantities from offshore depths in the winter. The inshore movement occurs in April, and there is good fishing into November, with most of the 3–6lb (1.3–2.7kg) jumbos being taken during the migratory movements, and often from deepwater wrecks. Juvenile sea bass are common around piers and bridges in bays during late summer.

DATA

Habitat: Inshore waters/wrecks/bays.

Habits: Bottom feeder.

Range: Cape Cod to northern Florida.

Size: Average ½–3lb (0.2–1.3kg), up to 10lb (4.5kg).

The black sea bass is a fish of many forms and colors. The small females are usually fairly slim and a rather bland mottled brownish color, while large males become stockier and a beautiful blue-black or indigo

with a prominent hump on the head, which may have white areas. Short, white fleshy tabs on the dorsal spines become more prominent in the males, and the white caudal fin lobes are elongated. Even in small sea bass, the upper and lower edges of the caudal fin are white, as are the outer edges of the dorsal and anal fins. As with the other serranids, sex reversal takes place in the black sea bass, with females becoming males as they grow older.

As far as eating qualities are concerned, there may be none better in northern waters than the black sea bass.

Tautog

Tautoga onitis

DATA
Habitat: Inshore waters/wrecks/bays.
Habits: Bottom feeder.
Range: Nova Scotia to South Carolina.
Size: Average 1–6lb (0.2–2.7kg), up to 25lb (11kg).

This very adaptable species is one of the most important bottom fish of the mid-Atlantic. The tautog and its cousin the cunner are the plain-colored northern members of the wrasse family Labridae, which is otherwise composed of colorful tropical species. Tautog is an Indian name, and it is used for this fish almost everywhere except the area from central New Jersey to New York, where the common name is black-fish. In the Chesapeake Bay area it may be nicknamed saltwater chub, oysterfish or black porgy. Though basically a coolwater fish, tautog thrive off the Virginia coast (where some of the largest have been caught and even survive in the warmth of North Carolina's Pamlico Sound, and Charleston Harbor, South Carolina. Yet, this fish (which is most abundant in southern New England and also common in Cape Cod Bay) doesn't inhabit many areas of the seemingly ideal rocky coast north of Cape Cod Canal – though a population exists all the way up in Eel Lake near Wedgeport, Nova Scotia.

There's no mistaking the tautog for any other fish. It's a stout fish with an unusually broad caudal peduncle and a caudal fin of almost similar width. Usually a mottled brown or black, the tautog has its spiny and soft dorsal fins connected, and sports a white chin and thick lips. It becomes active in inshore waters in May, but moves back to cooler depths by early summer before returning to rocky inshore areas and wrecks in the fall. Falling water temperatures late in autumn inspire a migration to more stable offshore depths, but some blackfish remain active on offshore banks, such as 17 fathoms off the North Jersey coast, throughout much of the winter.

This species has very firm white meat which is especially favored for chowder. The tough, oily skin should be stripped off.

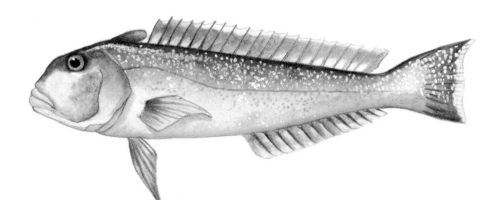

Tilefish

Lopholatilus chamaeleonticeps

DATA
Habitat: Offshore waters.
Habits: Bottom feeder.
Range: Nova Scotia to Florida, and eastern Gulf of Mexico.
Size: Average 3–20lb (1.3–9kg), up to 50lb (20kg).

This deepwater species exists in a very narrow band of water near the edge of the continental shelf. It is fished for primarily with bottom longlines, but overfishing has severely depleted the population in the prime areas from New Jersey to southern New England. A sportfishery existed in the 1960s and into the next decade, but once commercial fishing reduced the abundance it was no longer worthwhile for party boats to make the long trips offshore.

The story of the tilefish is a fascinating one, in that it was unknown to science until May, 1879, when a cod trawler landed 5,000lb taken south of Nantucket. The public had hardly become aware of the delicious eating quality of this species before vessels crossing the Atlantic spotted thousands of tilefish floating on the surface during the spring of 1882. This massive die-off was probably due to an invasion of cold water into the tilefish's restricted habitat of 47–53°F (8–12°C) bottom temperatures. So complete was the tragedy, that not a single tilefish was caught for another 10 years. However, the population rebounded to provide significant catches for the market in subsequent decades.

The colorful tilefish has a yellow-spotted upper body and a bright yellow fleshy tab on the head. The flesh is very firm and more like the lobsters and crabs they feed on than ordinary fish. Sportfishing for them involves the use of wire line or Dacron to eliminate stretch in the great depths. A small, whole squid makes an ideal bait.

This is one of the most abundant and underutilized species to be found along the mid-Atlantic coast. The striped searobin and the closely related northern searobin (*Prionotus carolinus*) are caught in vast numbers by anglers drifting for summer flounders in shallow inshore waters and bays from late spring well into the fall, but almost all are discarded because of their ugly appearance.

Searobins are instantly identified by the bony heads covered with sharp projections, the broad, wing-like pectoral fins, and three lower stiff, separate pectoral rays which seem to be used for feel on the bottom. The spines on the first dorsal are sharp,

Striped Searobin

Prionotus evolans

DATA

Habitat: Inshore waters/bays/surf.

Habits: Bottom feeder.

Range: Cape Cod to northern Florida.

Size: Average 1–2lb (0.45–0.9kg), up to 4lb (1.8kg) or more.

and this fish requires some care in handling. I prefer to grip them in the mouth, though that's more difficult with the relatively small mouth of the northern searobin. This species usually runs from 8–12in (20–30cm) in length and less than 1lb (0.45kg) in weight. It is basically a pest which is worth keeping only in the larger sizes. On the other hand, the striped searobin is a larger species with plenty of meat. Like its cousin, it will eat almost any bait presented. However, this species is quite game and will readily hit jigs and even large plugs.

Telling the two species apart is very easy. The northern searobin is slim with a non-descript dusky body, while the striped searobin has two or more dark stripes along the body with orange shading on the tips of the fins and the lower body.

The prime use of the striped searobin is as strip bait for summer flounders, but the white meat is actually very good eating when prepared in any manner. Similar species of the family Triglidae are considered gourmet fare in Europe.

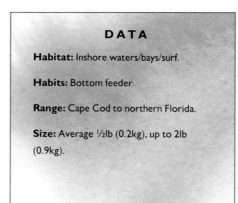

The puffer family, Tetraodontidae, consists primarily of small, very slow-moving fish which protect themselves from predators by inflating with water. Out of water they accomplish the same thing with air, and become so hard they can actually be bounced like a ball. The swelling ability leads to the common names of blowfish, swellfish, and globefish. However, it's scant protection for the juveniles who are a favorite of many predators, especially bluefish. Puffers have teeth which are fused to form a beak capable of crushing shellfish. They nibble at almost any bait and are

Northern Puffer

Sphoeroides maculatus

DATA

Habitat: Inshore waters/bays/surf.

Habits: Bottom feeder.

Range: Cape Cod to northern Florida.

Size: Average ½lb (0.2kg), up to 2lb (0.9kg).

expert bait stealers. Seemingly always hungry, schools of blowfish will often follow a hooked mate to the surface while trying to steal the bait hanging out of its mouth.

The puffer family produces a powerful poison, tetrodoxin, which is especially concentrated in their skin and internal organs. In most species, the meat may also be toxic. One species in this family is the delicacy known as *fugu* in Japan, where people die from eating it each year. Fortunately, the toxin levels in northern puffers are so low that you couldn't eat enough to suffer any ill effects. This species has a prickly skin which will scrape your hands in the cleaning process. Use gloves and cut through the backbone behind the head. Then push the meat forward by the tail and pull it free. What you're left with is solid, firm white meat with only a single backbone running through it. This delicious meat is sold in that form as sea squab or chicken of the sea, and can be prepared like a chicken leg.

Pacific Inshore Species

Species found along the inshore areas of the North American Pacific coast are different from those of the east and Gulf coasts, though many are members of the same families already reviewed. The striped bass was introduced from New Jersey a century ago, and is profiled in "Atlantic Coolwater Inshore Species". The Pacific bonito is similar to the Atlantic bonito (see page 67) and is a major game fish for Southern California party boats. The oceanic species were covered earlier.

LEFT: Author with a small yellowtail which hit a diamond jig.

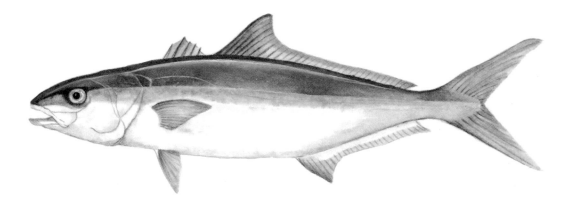

Yellowtail

Seriola lalandei

This is the only important member of the jack family Carangidae normally found in California waters. The roosterfish, Pacific amberjack and Pacific crevalle jack are fine game fish encountered in Baja California, and the jack mackerel (Trachurus symmetricus) is of some importance to commercial fishing, although it is utilized primarily as bait by sportfishers. Yellowtail have a body shape somewhat more elongate than that of the amberjack. The body color is metallic-blue to green above and silvery below, but with a light lemon-yellow stripe running along the median line into the all-yellow tail.

These voracious feeders are usually caught on live baits fished around kelp beds

DATA

Habitat: Inshore waters/kelp.

Habits: Mid to surface feeder.

Range: Central California to Baja California.

Size: Average 5–20lb (2.2–9kg), up to 80lb (36kg).

off southern California and the Baja California coast. San Diego party boats regularly make long-range trips down the Mexican coast to get into prime yellowtail fishing. Good California areas include the Coronado Islands, La Jolla Kelp, between Oceanside and Dana Pt, Horseshoe Kelp, Palos Verde Peninsula, Santa Catalina Island, and San Clemente Island. Trolling is also effective for yellowtails, and they'll frequently hit jigs worked at high speeds. An almost identical sub-species of yellowtail found on the other side of the Pacific averages twice the size, and the world record from New Zealand is a fish of 114lb 10oz (52kg).

Unlike many other jacks, the yellowtail is a fine table fish as well as a great gamester.

California Barracuda

Sphyraena argentea

DATA

Habitat: Inshore waters/kelp.

Habits: Mid to surface feeder.

Range: Magdalena Bay, Baja California to Pt Conception, California.

Size: 2–5lb (0.9–2.2kg), up to 20lb (9kg).

The only Pacific barracuda in North America is a small fish which rarely exceeds 10lb (45kg). They are caught in great numbers by party-boat anglers in southern California, and are one of the mainstays of that fishery.

This surface species feeds primarily on anchovies and other small fish, and is caught with similar live baits or by casting or trolling jigs and other lures. This brownish barracuda has a very slender and elongate body with no blotches on the body.

Whereas the much larger great barracuda of the Atlantic is often regarded as an inedible fish because it's so frequently associated with ciguatera poisoning, the California barracuda is a first-class food fish which carries no risks.

THE SCORPIONFISH FAMILY
Scorpaenidae

This large family includes about 400 species worldwide. These are divided in around 50 genera, with over 100 in the very important rockfish genus *Sebastes*. Though there are some Atlantic members of the family, the only one of commercial interest is the red-fish or ocean perch (*Sebastes marinus*).

The rockfishes range from the shallows out to great depths. These fish almost always have 13 stout spines in the dorsal fin, and are of great value as food. Fertilization and development of the embryo is internal, and live young are born.

Only two of the many Pacific rockfish are covered here. Others of some importance include the olive rockfish (*Sebastes serranoides*) of the California reefs and kelp beds; the greenspotted rockfish (*Sebastes chlorostictus*) of the depths; the colorful tiger rockfish (*Sebastes nigrocinctus*) of the Pacific Northwest; and the yelloweye rockfish (*Sebastes ruberrimus*) for which the IGFA recognizes a world record of 21¼lb (9.64kg) taken from Juan de Fuca Straits, Washington on April 26, 1988 by B Michael Schmidt.

Canary Rockfish

Sebastes pinniger

DATA

Habitat: Inshore to offshore waters.

Habits: Bottom feeder.

Range: Northern Baja California to northern British Columbia.

Size: Average 1–2lb (0.2–0.45kg) up to 12lb (5.4kg).

This excellent eating fish may be the most important of the family to commercial fishing. They are abundant in depths of 50–300ft (15–91m). This pretty species has orange body coloration with three bright orange stripes across the head, which has small spines. The lower jaw projects slightly, and is smooth to the touch – separating it from the vermillion rockfish. The fins are bright orange, and the lining of the mouth pale red. Canary rockfish smaller than 14in (35.5cm) have a black spot near the back of the first dorsal fin.

Blue Rockfish

Sebastes mystinus

This small, inshore rockfish is a schooling species very popular with anglers. It has a bass-like body and slate-blue coloration – though that can vary to olive brown or grayish-black. Blotches are present on the back and sides, but there are no spots on the dorsal fin and the tail is slanted or straight – characteristics which separate it from the similar black rockfish. (*Sebastes melanops*), which can grow to 12lb (5.5kg)

DATA

Habitat: Inshore waters/kelp.

Habits: All depths.

Range: Northern Baja California to the Bering Sea.

Size: ½–1 lb (0.2–0.45 kg), up to 4 lb (1.8 kg).

THE DRUM FAMILY
Sciaenidae

This large family of sound-emitting fishes includes such important Atlantic and Gulf species as the red drum, black drum, weakfish, spotted sea trout, and Atlantic croaker. However, there are also several species which are much sought after for sport and food in southern California. Included is the orangemouth corvina (*Cynoscion xanthulus*), a Gulf of California species which has been introduced successfully into California's inland Salton Sea, where it has been caught up to 37lb (16.7kg). Texas has tried crossing this species with the spotted seatrout, and the hybrid corvina has been caught up to 10½lb (4.7kg) in Calaveras Lake, San Antonio as of 1990.

White Seabass

Atractoscion nobilis

This is the giant of the drum family on the west coast. Unfortunately, the white seabass has been seriously overfished over the years and is both relatively hard to catch and much smaller on average than several decades ago – when 65,500 were caught on party boats in 1949 and 40-pounders (18kg) weren't uncommon. The longstanding IGFA all-tackle world record of 83¾lb (38kg) was caught at San Felipe, Mexico by L C Baumgardner on March 31, 1953, and it's unlikely to be broken in the near future. The white seabass name is one of the few misnomers which have been approved by the American Fisheries Society as a common name. This species looks nothing like a sea bass, but is more like a giant weakfish. However, it lacks the two enlarged, recurvate canine teeth. A raised ridge exists along the midline of the belly between the vent and the base of the ventral fins, and there's a black spot at the base of the pectoral fin. White seabass up to about 18in (45cm) have 3–6 broad, dark vertical bars on the sides, but

DATA

Habitat: Inshore waters/kelp.

Habits: Bottom to mid feeder.

Range: Magdalena Bay, Baja California to San Francisco.

Size: Average 7–15lb (3.1–6.8kg), up to 83¾lb (38kg).

these disappear with age. Usually found around kelp beds in depths of 12–25 fathoms from May to September, they also frequent deeper waters and come into the surf at times. Live anchovies and sardines are the usual baits, but live Pacific mackerel are the best bet for trophy fish, and live squid fished near bottom at night are consistent producers of white seabass. Lures should be fished slowly. In addition to kelp beds along the mainland, white seabass are likely to be found around Catalina and Clemente Islands, while the young often come into Santa Monica Bay. At the 28in (71cm) minimum length in California, white seabass weigh about 7½lb (3.4kg) and are five years old. They are long-lived fish, and 40-pounders (18kg) have been aged at about 20 years.

White seabass are good eating fish, but the meat is soft and spoils quickly.

California Corbina

Menticirrhus undulatus

This is the most sought-after species for southern California surfcasters. A delicious eating fish, the corbina was protected from netting in California in 1909, and from buying or selling in 1915. Similar to the northern, southern and Gulf kingfish of the Atlantic, the corbina is an elongate species with a long head, small mouth, and a single barbel on the chin. The body color is gray with incandescent reflections, and wavy diagonal lines on the sides. About 90 per cent of their diet consists of sand crabs, and soft-shells are the prime bait for them – though marine worms, mussels, ghost shrimp, and clams are also good. Sandy beaches from San Pedro to San Diego provide ideal corbina habitat, and San Onofre is considered a prime spot, with July to September being the best months.

DATA

Habitat: Surf/bays.

Habits: Bottom feeder.

Range: San Juanico Pt, Baja California to Pt Conception, California.

Size: Average ½–1½lb (0.2–0.6kg), up to 8½lb (3.8kg).

THE SURFPERCH FAMILY
Embiotocidae

This family of small fishes found in the surf along the west coast includes only a few species which exceed 12in (30cm) in length. All have roundish bodies with small mouths, and bear live young. They are fine-eating panfish which readily strike softshell sand crabs, mussels, marine worms, clams, and cut bait, as well as tiny lures and flies.

Barred Surfperch

Amphistichus argenteus

Most important is the barred surfperch (*Amphistichus argenteus*) which grows to 4½lb (2kg) and is the most common surf-caught species in southern California. It is distinguished from the similar calico and redtail surfperch by its lower jaw being shorter than the upper, and by the absence of reddish color on its fins. It is more common than other surfperch south of Cayucos, California, being most abundant on sandy beaches between Pt Mugu and Pismo Beach – and readily takes the same baits fished for corbina. The redtail surfperch (*Amphistichus rhodoterus*) can grow to 16in (40cm) and is most common from Bodega Bay, California north, with the Humboldt and Del Norte County, California, and Oregon coasts being prime areas. In addition to the red to deep purple tail, this species has a slight depression in the head above the eyes, and dorsal spines which are much longer than the soft rays. The calico surfperch (*Amphistichus koelzi*) has a spiny dorsal about as high as the soft rays plus numerous brown or brassy speckles forming irregular crossbars on the sides.

The rubberlip seaperch (*Rhacochilus toxotes*) grows to 18in (45cm) and about 4lb (1.8kg), and is found on sandy bottoms from central to southern California. Easily recognized by the thick lips, this species is taken in relatively large sizes from piers in the Monterey Bay area. The walleye surfperch (*Hyperprosopon argenteum*) may not even reach

DATA

Habitat: Inshore waters/surf.

Habits: Bottom feeder.

Range: Central California to Baja California.

Size: Average – less than 10in (25cm) up to 16in (40cm).

12in (30cm), but it's the most important portion of the commercial surfperch catch. They're the most abundant surfperch of the open rocky coast from central to southern California and are distinguished by the large eyes and black-tipped pelvic fins. Black surfperch (*Embiotoca jacksoni*) are highly coloured in olive-green to reddish brown, and feature about nine dark vertical bars on the sides, and thick orange-brown to yellow lips.

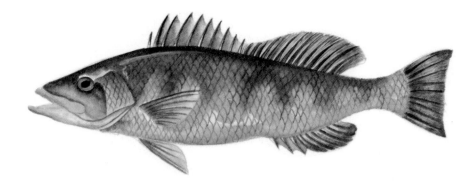

THE SEA BASS FAMILY
Serranidae

This is primarily an Atlantic family, including the groupers and black sea bass, but there are few important Pacific bass.

Kelp Bass

Paralabrax clathratus

DATA

Habitat: Inshore waters/kelp.

Habits: All depths.

Range: Magdalena Bay, Baja California to Columbia River, Washington.

Size: Average 1–2lb (0.45–0.9kg), up to 17lb (7.7kg).

Primarily encountered from Pt Conception, California to central Baja California, this fine sport fish is usually caught with live anchovies fished near the surface around kelp beds. They'll also hit many types of lures and dead bait. Kelp bass have a typical bass body, and are colored brown to olive green with light blotches. They can be distinguished from sand bass by the third dorsal fin which is about the same length as the fourth and fifth – rather than being much longer, as in the sand bass. Commercial fishing for kelp bass has been prohibited in California since 1953.

This relatively rare member of the temperate bass family Percichthyidae has been protected by a moratorium in California. Giant sea bass are very long-lived fish (a 435-pounder (197kg) was estimated to be 72–75 years old), but their relatively shallow offshore habitat makes them easy prey for divers. The IGFA world record 563½lb (225.8kg) giant sea bass taken at Anacapa Island, California by James D McAdam Jr on August 20, 1968 will probably stand for a long time to come. These

Giant Sea Bass

Stereolepis gigas

DATA

Habitat: Inshore waters.

Habits: Bottom feeder.

Range: Cabo San Lucas, Baja California to Pt Conception, California.

Size: Average 50–100lb (20–45kg); up to 600lb (272kg).

fish mature at between 11–13 years of age, when they weigh 50–60lb (20–27kg). Rocky bottoms in 10–25 fathoms, preferably near kelp beds, are ideal for giant sea bass – which are related to the striped bass and white perch rather than the somewhat similar jewfish, which is a grouper. Though no longer often hooked in California waters, some are caught with large live or dead baits fished off bottom from long range party boats out of San Diego as they work banks off Baja California.

Giant sea bass have more spines (11) than soft rays (9–10) in their dorsal fins, and the spines are shorter. The body is dark brown, and there are usually spots on the sides. The mouth is very large. Juvenile giant sea bass look quite different, being more perch-like in shape with brick-red sides featuring dark spots.

THE SCULPIN FAMILY
Cottidae

This huge family of generally small fish features a bony support beneath the eye, no spines in the anal fin, and the dorsal fin deeply notched between the spiny and soft portions. Most have broad, flat heads and winglike pectoral fins. Over 100 species are found in North America, including many tiny freshwater sculpins and a large represent-ation in the North Pacific. The Pacific stag-horn sculpin (*Leptocottus armatus*) is a small inshore species, rarely exceeding 12in (30cm), which is found from California to Alaska and even into fresh waters. Spines on the gill covers can produce nasty cuts, and this fish isn't valued for sport or food – but is used for striped bass bait in the San Francisco Bay Delta. The red Irish lord (*Hemilepidotus hemilepidotus*) grows to 1½ft (45cm) in cooler Pacific waters and features white and purplish red spots on its olive-green body. The great sculpin (*Myoxocephalus polyacanthocephalus*) is found from Washing-ton to the Bering Sea at moderate depths, and grows to 30in (76cm). It has fleshy papillae scattered over the body, with a pale band crossing the dark olive to black body, with black markings on all but the pelvic fins.

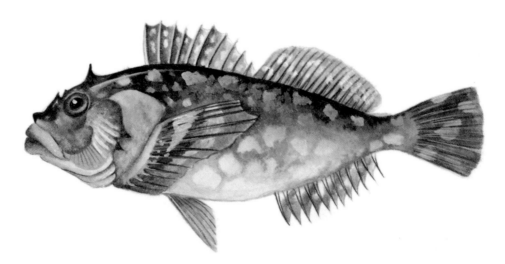

Cabezon

Scorpaenichthys marmoratus

DATA

Habitat: Inshore waters/kelp.

Habits: Bottom feeder.

Range: Northern Baja California to Sitka, Alaska.

Size: Average 2–5lb (0.9–2.2kg); up to 25lb (11kg).

The largest of the sculpins is a highly esteemed food and sport fish taken prim-arily in shallow, rocky waters averaging 35ft (10m) – though they range from tide pools to 250ft (76m). They are bottom fish which will readily respond to cut baits and jigs. The color is highly variable, with females usually more greenish in hue and males more red. It has no scales on the body, and has flaps of skin over the eyes and in the middle of the snout.

Though the meat may have a bluish-green color, it turns white when cooked and is excellent for frying. However, the roe is poisonous.

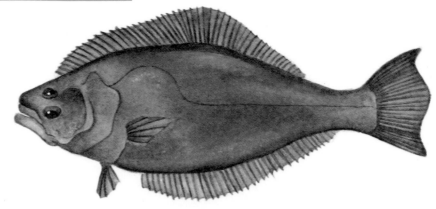

THE LEFT-EYE FLOUNDERS
Bothidae

In this portion of the order Pleuronecti-formes, flounders who begin life looking like ordinary fish start leaning to the right – and the right eye moves to the left side of the body. Most left-eyed flounders are Atlantic species, including the very important summer, southern and gulf flounders.

California Halibut

Paralichthys californicus

DATA

Habitat: Inshore waters.

Habits: Bottom feeder.

Range: Magdalena Bay, Baja California to Klamatth River, California.

Size: Average 2–10lb (0.9–4.5kg); up to 72lb (32kg).

Ironically, this left-handed flounder is right-handed over 40 per cent of the time! However, it can be distinguished from all other California flounders by the large mouth with numerous sharp teeth plus a high arch in the lateral line above the pectoral fin. Sandy bottoms in less than 10 fathoms are the usual habitat, but California halibut also frequent the channels of Morro Bay and Mission Bay. They even enter the surf at times. Drift fishing with live baits is effective for this species, but they also hit jigs at times.

THE RIGHT-EYE FLOUNDERS
Pleuronectidae

These flounders have both eyes on the right side of the body. Pacific members dominate the family, though the important winter flounder, yellowtail flounder and Atlantic halibut are found on the east coast. Several species with the name "sole" are included in this family, but aren't true soles of the family *soleidae*. The petrale sole (*Eopsetta jordani*) is a northern offshore species that grows to 8lb (3.6kg) and features a somewhat pointed snout with a lateral line which curves upward over the pectoral fin on the olive-brown eyed side. Also known as the brill, it is a rough-scaled flounder. The Dover sole (*Microstomus pacificus*) is another large off shore flounder, reaching 10lb (4.5kg). It has a heavy slime covering the body plus large eyes, a small mouth and a straight lateral line.

Pacific Halibut

Hippoglossus stenolepis

DATA

Habitat: Inshore to offshore waters.

Habits: Bottom feeder.

Range: Santa Rosa Island, California to the Bering Sea.

Size: Average 10–100lb (4.5–45kg); up to over 500lb (227kg).

This huge flatfish has a high arch in the lateral line over the pectoral fin and a lunate caudal fin. The lower jaw extends to the front edge of the eye, whereas in the California halibut it extends beyond the eye. Most Pacific halibut caught in northern California are taken in nearshore areas, but they're found in greater depths to the north. This very valuable species has long been regulated by international agreement between the US and Canada, and this has helped stabilize the population.

Diamond Turbot

Hypsopsetta guttulata

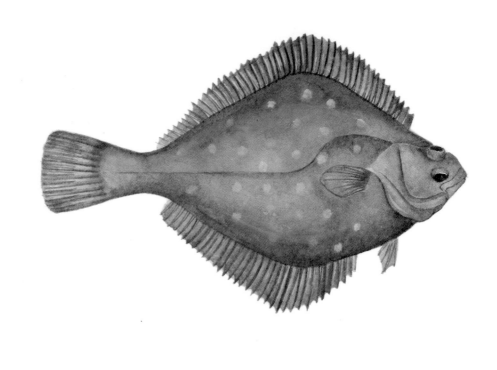

DATA

Habitat: Inshore waters/bays/rivers.

Habits: Bottom feeder.

Range: Cabo San Lucas, Baja California to Cape Mendocino, California.

Size: Average ½lb (0.2kg); up to 4lb (1.8kg).

The eyed side of this diamond-shaped flounder is green with pale blue spots, and its underside is white with a lemon-yellow patch around the mouth. They favor muddy or sandy bottoms in bays and sloughs, and are caught year-round with small pieces of clam or shrimp in such areas as Mission Bay and Newport Bay.

Starry Flounder

Platichthys stellatus

DATA

Habitat: Inshore waters/bays/rivers.

Habits: Bottom feeder.

Range: Pt Arguello, California to the Aleutian Islands.

Size: Average 1–3lb (0.45–1.3kg); up to 20lb (9kg).

Though a member of the right-eyed flounder family, the vast majority of starry flounders are actually left-handed. These are the most common flatfish in northern California, and are very popular in San Francisco Bay and from area beaches. They're most abundant there from December through March, and will hit chunks of sardine, clam, shrimp, squid, and worm. They're also very important in inshore areas further north, and have ascended the Columbia River as far as 75 miles (120km) upstream. These fish are easily recognized by the alternating pattern of orange-white and dark bars on the fins, the small mouth, and nearly straight lateral line. The dark brown body is rough on the eyed side.

California Sheepshead

Semicossyphus pulcher

This is the only important member of the wrasse family on the west coast, and a very unusual species. They begin life as females and become males later in life – usually at about 12in (30cm) and 7–8 years. The females are a uniform pinkish red with a white lower jaw, but males become black on the head and rear third of the body, while the midsection remains red and the lower jaw is still white. A fatty hump develops on the head during the breeding season of this long-lived species. The large

> **DATA**
>
> **Habitat:** Inshore waters.
>
> **Habits:** Bottom feeder.
>
> **Range:** Cabo San Lucas, Beja California to Monterey Bay, California.
>
> **Size:** Average 2–5lb (0.9–2.2kg); up to 40lb (18kg).

mouth features canine teeth for feeding on shellfish, but they'll also take fish baits and even hit jigs on occasion. Most California sheepshead are caught from rocky kelp areas 20–100ft (6–30m) deep. The firm, white flesh is excellent eating.

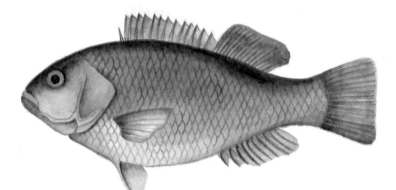

Opaleye

Girella nigricans

The most important Pacific representative of the sea chub family Kyphosidae, the opaleye may be the only basically vegetarian fish actively sought by anglers. They live along rocky shorelines and in kelp beds primarily south of Pt Conception. Though they browse on both plant and animal matter, the larger fish tend to subsist on more of the former. As a result, anglers often use moss as bait for this difficult-to-hook and hard-fighting species. The opaleye is easily recognized by its oval and compressed body, dark olive green color, bright blue eyes, and one or two white spots on

> **DATA**
>
> **Habitat:** Surf/kelp.
>
> **Habits:** Bottom feeder.
>
> **Range:** Cabo San Lucas, Beja California to Monteray Bay, California.
>
> **Size:** Average 1–2lb (0.45–0.9kg); up to 13½lb (6kg).

each side of the back under the dorsal fin of most individuals. Opaleye anglers also catch another member of the family, the halfmoon (*Medialuna californiensis*). This fish is so named due to the half-moon shape of its tail. The bluish body is oval and compressed, while the head is blunt and rounded. They're most common in southern California, particularly around the Channel Islands.

This small, excellent eating fish may grow to 5lb (2.2kg), and is more likely to be caught on mussels, shrimp, and cut bait than the opaleye.

Sablefish

Anoplopoma fimbria

DATA

Habitat: Offshore waters.

Habits: Bottom feeder.

Range: California to the Bering Sea.

Size: Average 5–10lb (2.2–4.5kg); up to 56lb (25kg).

This blackish gray, elongate fish with two, well-separated dorsal fins is caught primarily by commercial fishers in offshore waters from northern California to Alaska. Though usually found on sandy bottoms in depths of 450ft (137m) or more, young sablefish often school in inshore waters during the summer. They are caught by bottom fishing, and aren't great fighters. However, the oily white meat is excellent for smoking.

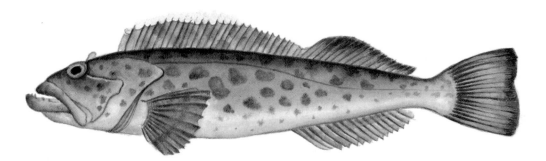

This species has become more popular over the years with sportfishers. It's caught primarily north of central California, but the Coronodos Islands also produce significant numbers. This offshore member of the greenling family Hexagrammidae lives at or near the bottom in rocky areas and kelp beds. Though most abundant at depths to 350ft (106m), they often occur near shore in northern areas.

The long body shape with a large toothy

Lingcod

Ophiodon elongatus

DATA

Habitat: Inshore to offshore waters.

Habits: Bottom feeder.

Range: California to Alaska.

Size: Average 5–20lb (2.2–9kg); up to 70lb (31kg).

mouth and dark blotches over the head and body distinguish this fish. The long dorsal fin is continuous, but deeply notched between the spiny and soft-rayed portions. Lingcod feature sharp gillrakers as well as teeth, and care must be taken in handling them. Live bait is the best bet, but dead baits and jigs will also work for lingcod.

Their excellent eating flesh has a greenish tint which disappears when it's cooked.

Index

Page reference may be to text and/or illustrations. Those to main identification entry in bold.

Acknowledgements

Photographs © Al Ristori

Illustrations: Sharon Bailey, Student from the School of Illustration Bournemouth and Poole College of Art and Design